BIBLICAL STORYTELLING DESIGN

"Human beings love stories. We love to hear them and tell them. Our stories shape who we are. Over the past few decades, evangelists, Bible teachers, and church planters have discovered the importance and art of telling stories in ministry. In this new book, Jim Roché adds to this momentum by presenting a practical guide for gospel storytelling that will equip cross-cultural workers as well people ministering within their home cultures. I recommend it."

—Edward L. Smither, Dean, Professor of Intercultural Studies,
Columbia International University

"Jim Roché's well-researched and thoroughly field-tested model not only helps us understand *why* we must appreciate story form but also *how* we must understand and apply best practices and avoid common fatal flaws associated with its use among people for whom story form is crucial to their literacy level and central to their cultural fabric. It is essential reading for those of us who are passionate not merely to broadcast biblical truth but instead to instill and perpetuate it on behalf of global church multiplication."

—Ralph E. Enlow Jr., President,
Association for Biblical Higher Education

"As a doctor of education who is well versed in principles of pedagogy, Jim Roché provides a professional handling of storytelling, especially in oral cultures, that is second to none. This fresh look at biblical storytelling provides practical ways to craft oral biblical stories and lessons that are applicable to any culture. Roché expertly weaves the how and why of storytelling through step-by-step considerations that ultimately leads to effective curriculum design, which in turn leads to effective communication of biblical truth."

—Marvin J. Newell, Senior Vice President, Missio Nexus

"Dr. Jim Roché helps give a broader understanding, beyond storytelling, of the multiple aspects of the orality movement. I believe his book can be a great tool, not only for those who are new to orality and biblical story telling, but also to those who are advanced practitioners. I highly recommend Jim's book to anyone interested in the Great Commission and pray that it receives wide distribution."

—Jerry Wiles, North America Regional Director, International Orality Network; President Emeritus, Living Water International

"The reader will quickly sense the passion Dr. Roché has for storytelling. His experience, research, and practiced educational principles make this book a valuable tool for both the beginner and veteran storyteller. An educator at heart, the author leads the reader through a process whereby this ancient art form becomes a powerful means for communicating truth, a form which encourages reflection, absorption, and incorporation into patterns of obedience. Structured use of story breathes life into teaching and quickens life in listeners."

—Duane H. Elmer, Distinguished Professor of Educational Studies Emeritus, G. W. Aldeen Professor of International Studies (Retired), Trinity International University

"When our church planters forge rivers, cross rugged terrain, or scale mountains to reach previously unreached people groups with the gospel of God's redeeming grace, they will inevitably encounter communities of predominantly non-literate families. How can they communicate the written word of God to those who cannot read—and in a way that helps those same people communicate to their own cultural network, in a manner familiar to them? . . . This book explains how to leave witnesses who have that story indelibly recorded in their hearts and minds."

—Peter W. Law, President, ENGAGE International

"Jim Roché has used his formal learning and doctoral understanding of education and curriculum planning to teach us through this excellent book how to become storytellers ourselves—to tell stories like our grandparents and culture did, with a moral so that we may pass on to others how to live. I strongly encourage colleagues, friends, and especially fellow educators to use this excellent book to teach their students how to teach effectively."

—Junias Venugopal, Associate Dean, School of Mission, Ministry, and Leadership, Wheaton College

BIBLICAL STORYTELLING DESIGN

Understanding Why Oral Stories Work

Jim Roché

Foreword by J. O. Terry

WIPF & STOCK · Eugene, Oregon

BIBLICAL STORYTELLING DESIGN
Understanding Why Oral Stories Work

Copyright © 2020 Jim Roché. All rights reserved. Except for brief quotations in critical publications or reviews, no part of this book may be reproduced in any manner without prior written permission from the publisher. Write: Permissions, Wipf and Stock Publishers, 199 W. 8th Ave., Suite 3, Eugene, OR 97401.

Wipf & Stock
An Imprint of Wipf and Stock Publishers
199 W. 8th Ave., Suite 3
Eugene, OR 97401

www.wipfandstock.com

PAPERBACK ISBN: 978-1-7252-5811-2
HARDCOVER ISBN: 978-1-7252-5812-9
EBOOK ISBN: 978-1-7252-5813-6

Manufactured in the U.S.A.   APRIL 6, 2020

Portions reprinted with permission from *Learning to Listen, Learning to Teach: The Power of Dialogue in Educating Adults*, by Jane Vella. San Francisco: Jossey-Bass, 1994.

Portions reprinted with permission from *Resonate: Present Visual Stories that Transform Audiences*, by Nancy Duarte. Hoboken, NJ: Wiley and Sons, 2010.

Portions reprinted and used with permission from *The Insanity of God: A True Story of Faith Resurrected*, by Nik Ripken. Nashville, TN: B&H, 2013.

Scripture quotations taken from the New American Standard Bible® (NASB), copyright © 1960, 1962, 1963, 1968, 1971, 1972, 1973, 1975, 1977, 1995 by The Lockman Foundation. Used by permission. www.Lockman.org

Table of Contents

Foreword by J. O. Terry ix
Acknowledgments xi
Introduction xiii
The Design of This Book xv

PART 1: CRAFTING BIBLICAL STORYTELLING

Chapter 1: The Process of Creating Story Lessons 3
    Misconceptions Are Essential to the Story 4
    Identify the Main Points 8
    Identify the Biblical Passage 9
    Craft the Story 10
    Developing Questions 14
    Selecting Scripture Memory Verses 19
    Selecting the "Hook Question" 20
    Chapter Summary 20
Chapter 2: Creating Story Lesson Sets 22
    Chapter Summary 28

PART 2: COUNTERING SEVEN NEGATIVE INFLUENCES AFFECTING STORYING

Chapter 3: The Influence of Mismatched Teaching and Learning Preferences 31
    Oral and Literate Learners Process Information Differently 33
    Oral Preference Learners Are Everywhere; Local and Foreign 34
    Biblical Models Supporting Oral Teaching to Oral Learners 36
    Strategic Implications of Oral Storying 42
    Education Requirements for Teaching Stories 45
    Chapter Summary 46

Table of Contents

Chapter 4: The Influence of the Listener's Own Worldview 48
    Worldview and Conceptual Formation 49
    Forming Information into Concepts 50
    Building Values into a Worldview 55
    Social Construction of Worldviews 57
    The Influence of Words in Constructing Worldview and Stories 57
    Changing Misconceptions Within a Worldview 62
    Conceptual Change Teaching Strategy 63
    Use Caution When Identifying Others' Perspectives as Misconceptions 68
    Chapter Summary 69
Chapter 5: The Influence of the Storyteller Assuming the Role of Teacher 70
    The Hebrew Understanding of Teaching 72
    The Role of the Storyteller 73
    Creating the Environment for Adult Learning 74
    Chapter Summary 77
Chapter 6: The Influence of Addition Instead of Multiplication Processes 78
    Discerning Addition or Multiplication Processes 80
    Educational Design and Multiplication 83
    The Impact of Dependent Resources Limiting Multiplication 84
    Chapter Summary 85
Chapter 7: The Influence of Restricting Movement Growth 86
    Connecting with Friends in Relational Networks 87
    Creating a Movement 91
    Negative Influences Affecting Movement Strategy 93
    Why Storytelling Is a Remedy 96
    Chapter Summary 99
Chapter 8: The Influence of Diverse Beliefs and Practices within the Community 100
    Developing Spiritual Habits 102
    Develop Community Culture through Community Habits 102
    Peer Pressure as Persecution or Accountability 105
    Chapter Summary 108
Chapter 9: The Influence of Leadership Using Local but Unbiblical Criteria 110
    Storytelling and Leadership Development 113
    Chapter Summary 115

TABLE OF CONTENTS

PART 3: IMPLEMENTING CURRICULUM DESIGN REMEDIES

Chapter 10: Design Elements that Counteract Negative Influences 119
    The Relationship of Curriculum Design and Story Lessons 122
    Chapter Summary 125
Chapter 11: Teaching This Approach to Others 126
    The Two Groups in Your Generational Lineage 126
    Identifying Your Listener Target Groups 130
    Final Words 133

Bibliography 135
Scripture Index 137

Foreword

I KNOW JIM ROCHÉ personally and we have shared ideas and communicated frequently. I was immediately impressed by his thirst for understanding oral Bible story methodology, which was continuing to spread among those on the mission field planting churches, discipling new believers, and even among those working with oral learners in the U.S. His many questions opened doors for sharing about orality experiences and current Bible Storying methodology. Jim was proving to be a fast learner, grasping concepts that Bible storying pioneers had struggled to work out through trial and error while lacking a thorough understanding of effective curriculum development as a key part of Bible Storying strategy.

Jim shares his curriculum insights in a practical way that pioneer Bible storyers can use to be effective in their teaching and training of oral learners. The learning curve for literate missionaries can be steep and humbling as they transition from using generic model sets of Bible story lessons originally developed for other peoples to specific effective curricula for teaching and training oral learners and oral-preference learners among each different people group.

When Jim first shared some of his thinking I was immediately impressed with the possibility of bringing order out of the collected shared experiences by applying the principles of practical curriculum development from a rationale and understanding that many Bible Storying pioneers lacked. Jim has kept orality in view while expressing practical concepts for literate workers.

My first and only regret is having connected with Jim in retirement from the mission field. At one point I wondered, "Where was Jim Roché when I was first drawn into using oral-friendly curriculum with village folks?"

Foreword

I personally appreciate the practicality of Jim's writing and his patience in sharing with me, and being available so that others can become competent in developing effective curricula through a process that looks at avoiding common mistakes literates can make when preparing to teach and train oral learners.

His text is comprehensive and thorough, simple to understand, and highly applicable to anyone developing and using Bible Storying methodology to teach new believers and train emerging oral leaders.

J. O. Terry

Acknowledgments

THE CONTENTS OF THIS book are the result of others' contributions to my life and ministry, beginning with Chuck Lloyd who led me to understand faith in Jesus Christ my Savior. Then Chuck and his wife, Barbara, invited me into their family for two years to learn about discipleship.

I then studied four years at Dallas Theological Seminary, leaving with a passion for the Bible and Christian education, particularly nurtured by the late Dr. Howard Hendricks.

Following seminary, I accepted a call to serve as Pastor of Christian Education at Church of the Open Door in York, Pennsylvania. This amazing church offered patience, love, and opportunities for me to teach and serve—even years later when they became my sending church when I became a missionary.

I left the pastorate to study education at Trinity International University in their doctoral program. This is where I learned to love academic research, and disciplined inquiry from both the late Dr. Ted Ward and Dr. Perry Downs, who supervised my doctoral research on educational strategies to challenge worldview. Portions of this book emerged from that research.

The next fourteen years, I served in higher education administration at Columbia International University, where I was greatly affected by the passion of its missions ethos that drove both the professors and the students.

That influence propelled me into missionary service for the next seventeen years with two agencies, the last years of which I served with Entrust as their director of the Southern European Orality Project which refined and validated my thinking into this book. This project was a new initiative enthusiastically supported by Entrust. My colleague, Norma A., took my theories and we experimented and refined our thoughts as she served

Acknowledgments

among refugees. We have since trained other missionaries and agencies in the strategies of this book.

So this book is the result of others who lovingly poured into me personal discipleship, the love of Scripture, critical inquiry, and missions. It has been seasoned with the practical support and love from my financial and prayer support team along with Entrust, who trusted and encouraged me as I experimented, wrote, and edited. Also appreciated was the timely and wise encouragements of Dr. Steve Hoke of NOVO and my experienced and gifted friend J. O. Terry. Throughout the entire journey, there has been the patience and encouragement of my wife, Winnie, and son, Kevin. To all of you, my thanks.

But the greatest joy of the process were times when the Holy Spirit, the Author of the Book, brought unity to my thoughts, and realizations of connections that I knew were not from the significant limitations of my own mind. Therefore, the gift of this book is returned as an offering to my God.

Introduction

JESUS DID NOT TELL stories to pass on information in an entertaining way. Jesus told stories because he wanted his listeners to change how they viewed themselves and their world.

Stories can do that. They can unlock the imagination of the listeners to consider alternative explanations or meaning for their life experiences by comparing their lives with the characters and events from the stories and fables they hear. Hearing stories can engage creativity to bring about understanding or change in listeners' lives. We can never change another person's understanding of how the world works because each of us is the creator of our own worldview and, consequently, the only ones who can change it. But by hearing stories and experiences through stories, we can discover alternative insights and experiences in a safe, controlled environment that might provide greater success, clarity, and understanding of our world. Skilled storytellers, through well-crafted stories, provide the setting and motivation for listeners to discover, reflect, and change their own perspectives and interpretations of life. Stories are that powerful . . . if they are crafted, or told, for such purposes.

That's what this book is about; offering ways to craft biblical stories that engage the listeners' minds and begin new generations of disciples who can continue to retell the stories and lessons and thereby bring changes to their own lives and, eventually, their communities. There are, however, negative influences that can hinder the process. But the good news is that these hindrances can be overcome by applying educational design principles in the story-crafting process.

Several years ago, I was asked to develop an education curriculum to improve a mission agency's training program to multiply spiritual generations of churches among people who had little or no access to the gospel in hostile environments. I had a blank computer screen and a blank mind

Introduction

staring at it, and I grew more anxious as I tried to think more deeply but wasn't getting the answers I needed. I had slipped into confusing what was strategic and what was methodological when two statements and a question came to mind with unusual power and authority:

> Curriculum is not a strategy.
> Curriculum supports the strategy.
> What is your strategy?

After months of reflection and discussions with my friends, I returned with increased commitment to the Apostle Paul's strategy he taught his disciple, Timothy: "The things you have heard from me in the presence of many witnesses . . . " identifies the first two generations of ministry outreach: Paul and Timothy. But Paul continued his command, " . . . entrust these to faithful men who will be able to teach others also" (2 Timothy 2:2). Those are the third and fourth generations and where multiplication comes into play. Multiplication is the structure that forms as spiritual generations develop.

Paul identified *faithfulness* as the critical character trait and *the ability to teach* as the critical skill that determines the success or failure of the preceding generations' hope to continue a spiritual legacy. Without faithfulness and skill to teach the next generation, there remains a cycle and recycle limited to only the first two generations. This is why exhausted first-generation evangelists don't always see multiplying generations from their efforts. Multiplication can't happen until the next generation demonstrates faithfulness and the ability to teach a new generation that *replaces* the work of the first evangelist. That's the strategic structural target that must be built. The building process is dependent on the ability of new believers to teach the next generation.

That's an immense amount of responsibility and expectation placed on a new believer, who can only pass on what had been personally experienced and modeled by another who learned it from the previous generation. That leads to asking, "the ability to teach . . . what?"

A foundational principle of good education is that it is "learner centered" rather than "teacher centered." Effective teaching is not about how the teacher prefers to teach, but how the listener prefers to learn. Jesus' examples and Paul's strategy are dependent upon *new* converts reaching *their* friends—not dependent on mature theologians and defenders of the faith from previous generations. *What* to teach is clear: only God's Scripture is

Introduction

authoritative: "All scripture is inspired by God and profitable for teaching, for reproof, for correction, for training in righteousness; so that the man of God may be adequate, equipped for every good work" (2 Tim 3:16, 17). The challenge of Paul's strategy is its dependence upon new converts being "able to teach" in such a way that causes others to view themselves and their world differently and yet requires the content of their teaching to be simple and uncomplicated to support repetition to others. The answer proposed here is not to require the new convert to teach theological truths, but rather to tell biblical stories and encourage discussion. The meat of theology cannot be expected to be taught by new converts and therefore should be postponed for the mature believers when they emerge.

The Design of This Book

This book provides practical ways to craft oral biblical stories and lessons. Yes, it is possible for stories to be told too casually and discussions unplanned and pointless that results in limited influence. Though there are several practical books about oral storytelling, this book is unique because 1) it provides a seven-part lesson format based upon a story; 2) it identifies seven potentially negative influences that—unless intentionally counteracted by educational decisions—will limit or even halt spiritual generations, 3) it will identify and integrate sound educational philosophy and psychology with relevant anthropological and sociological insights, 4) it will keep all these insights balanced and focused on mission objectives, and 5) it will offer analysis of many biblical examples of stories to encourage your confidence in using storytelling as a powerful tool honored by God. This book's contribution is not just to tell you *how* to be effective, but *why* oral biblical storytelling is both effective and strategic. Therefore, the book is divided into three parts.

Part 1 presents a foundational story lesson format. Each of the seven parts of this lesson format are briefly and simply described as a framework and shape for the end goal of multiplying spiritual generations of story crafters and tellers who are faithful and equipped to repeat stories to their relationship networks. Recognizing the impact of telling several related stories instead of just one story is supported by grouping stories into sets of stories to reinforce their common theme from different biblical stories and characters.

Introduction

Part 2 identifies seven potential negative influences, or hindrances that can limit or even terminate our objective of continuing spiritual generations. These seven influences affect three critical battlegrounds—educational strategy, reproduction strategy, and community strategy—that affect the foundational story lesson format. These three strategic areas expose weaknesses that must be addressed by decisions made by curriculum design.

Therefore, educational remedies are proposed that counter those influences. All seven countering remedies reinforce each other to shape a simple and reproducible approach using biblical storytelling. The way the story is crafted and told affects multiplication strategy, spiritual growth, and community development. In turn, the faith community's impact upon the society is strengthened by its own people retelling God's stories over and over to provide a spiritual identity and suggest solutions informed by the experiences of the Bible.

Part 3 identifies curriculum design decisions that purposefully refine and direct not only the story itself, but the way it is presented and the strategies that cause the listener to engage with the lesson. If the word "curriculum" didn't make your mind soar and your heart beat faster, then the good news for you is that it is not *that* curriculum—the first thought that came to your mind with accompanying thoughts of "boring," "irrelevant," "technical" or "syllabus." If you thought about printed words when you thought curriculum, then no—this is the other one. And if you thought storytelling was just one more way to provide entertaining and easily memorized information to pass on to others, then no again—this is the other one. And if you thought this would be about outlines and condensed conclusions, then it's not that one either—it's the other one. So what remains in your thoughts that could be the *other* curriculum—the one that didn't generate a negative response?

First consider that the word for "curriculum" can also be translated as "path." That path includes everything around it. Education is not a "pure" discipline but built upon sociological, psychological, and anthropological foundations that provide more questions to ask from different perspectives to answer the question of how people learn. This allows us to generate more observations and discoveries resulting in more insight, opportunities, and solutions. So education and curriculum design will guide us toward enabling third-generation faithful people to be able to teach others also. That's our goal.

Introduction

A former colleague used to say, "The faculty is the curriculum." That's good. Curriculum is not just printed material; it's everything from the teacher—no, let's stop with the role divisions between teachers and students—it's *everyone* and *everything* along the path that can cause learning. Since we can learn from fellow students or practitioners, *everyone* is both a teacher *and* a learner. Teachers, colleagues, and peers are part of your curriculum—your path. Everything is available for you to analyze on that path. That's a large amount of information to create meaning to understand this world! How our minds are able to do that is discussed in chapter 4. The curriculum design exists to support Paul's strategy and blunt the negative influences that intentionally or unintentionally work against the strategy.

You are encouraged to make your own path or curriculum. This book simply points out the passing scenery and offers vistas of hills and valleys with encouragements and warnings along the way. But you make the choice; you make the discoveries that will improve your evangelism and discipleship ministries. Your path is in your country or community, which is different than mine. There will be different emphases that should be reflected and specific to your context, but the destination is the same—to reach the world for Christ's glory through enabling one another. Enjoy the trip, enjoy your path, and welcome to the ministry of telling God's stories from one generation to another as the psalmist said, "One generation shall praise Your works to another and shall declare Your mighty acts" (Ps 145:4). It's the next generation's time to hear from you.

Part 1

Crafting Biblical Storytelling

Chapter 1

The Process of Creating Story Lessons

AN ORAL STORY IS not the same as an oral *lesson*; the story is only one of seven parts to an oral lesson. There is a process and order in developing or crafting each of these parts. A critical goal of the lesson is to create discussions about the story between the storyteller and the listener so the listener discovers and owns the conclusion—meaning the listener has rejected a deficient personal belief or attitude to adopt a new belief or perspective discovered in the story through these discussions and personal reflection. As powerful as that objective is, the lesson must still be crafted to be so simple and relatable that it can be retold almost immediately by the listener to another friend, regardless if the listener was a Christian or not. These seven components are

1. Misconceptions
2. Main Points
3. Biblical Passage
4. Story
5. Questions
6. Scripture Memory
7. Hook Question

There are several advantages to crafting the parts in the same order as listed. When using a consistent approach, the process is more easily passed along to the next generation of storytellers or lesson crafters as they hopefully produce new stories to meet the needs within their own culture. The process will likely lead to a consistent story form and style that becomes familiar to the listeners and helps develop their new identity as "tellers of the story." Following the same process protects the story crafter from skipping steps that are likely critical to the lesson and helps the story crafter become more efficient and answer the nagging question about what to do next. However, when the inevitable mental block happens while building the story, try brainstorming ideas out of sequence to gain a fresh, new perspective before returning to the step.

It is impossible to read the gospels without being amazed at the humility of Jesus Christ. He always approached others with a balanced response whereas his accusers always tried to approach him from a position of power, authority, and knowledge. Whether entering a new community or approaching an individual, our approach should reflect the same level of respect and love as Jesus. This balanced approach of telling a story changes the dynamic from one person telling another what they don't know or can't understand—which subtly or unintentionally communicates a position of power over another—to a dynamic of two people discussing characters and event plots about a shared story that doesn't have a personal relationship to either person. That dynamic deflects the engagement from direct questioning of each other in a win or lose power argument to discussions about the characters' responses to life that encourages creating discovery of very relevant implications. But how do you create stories that create such a non-threatening atmosphere where such discoveries of relevance can be realized? The answer is found at the very beginning of the story's design purpose: the misconception.

Misconceptions Are Essential to the Story

There are at least three reasons why crafting a story from the initial perspective of the listeners' misconception(s) gives the advantage to the storyteller.

1. It creates a common point of relevance for both the listener and the storyteller.
2. It creates an expectation of learning more about something already familiar to the listener.
3. It creates a feeling of curiosity that encourages exploring and questioning conclusions already accepted.

The Process of Creating Story Lessons

It's an extremely difficult task to get listeners engaged in your story if it seems irrelevant to them. The listener first thinks, "What has this got to do with me? I'm not interested in this! This is a waste of my time!" You prefer listeners' responses to be more like, "This is interesting to hear because I think I know something about this; I can relate to this person and this story . . . " The best response would be, "I'm working through the exact problem right now. How did this other person solve it?"

Notice how Jesus *always* presented a story relevant to the listeners. He picked up on their conversations or situations; they were already involved in the topic in some manner. The first rule of any speaking opportunity is *to know your audience*. Jesus never told a story that was irrelevant. So too, we need to identify what misconception might be revealed in our conversations. That guides the storyteller to select the story and introduce it naturally with a phrase like, "I know a story that deals with some of the concerns we've been talking about. Would you be interested in hearing it?"

To be developed in greater detail in chapter 4, misconceptions are misunderstandings or misperceptions of how the world works (including both the physical and the spiritual realms). Misconceptions develop from either inaccurate conclusions following reflection of experiences or inaccurate community values and behaviors often reinforced through public rituals, holidays, and schooling. Therefore, these are the places where the storyteller should begin to look for the presence of misconceptions. Studying the culture or listening to the casual words of the person in conversation provides telltale clues to the story crafter to relate in a relevant way to a biblical worldview's perspective. Beginning a story that begins with a different perspective from a listener's misconception is an engaging introduction! The goal of the story is not simply to transfer information like a full bucket to an empty bucket, but to create an opportunity for the listener to discover and adopt a different perspective.

Evangelists do more than present the gospel or biblical story to the person standing before them; they are also modeling to the listener how that person can tell their friends. Though it might not be the intention of the evangelist, that's the model that the person will most likely use later. If the model is a teaching approach with an elegant defense of the Christian faith, the model is certainly beyond the new converts' comfort level or theological capabilities. It's a model that won't immediately multiply from the first generation; the process is already slowed down to wait for the convert to be sufficiently trained and mature even though our reproduction strategy calls for a new believer to reach his or her friends as quickly as possible.

But if the model is telling and discussing a story together, then new converts can begin to tell others immediately. That's why, when entering a new community, the storyteller should resist the temptation to immediately begin telling favorite and familiar stories unavoidably influenced by the storyteller's own past influences. Rather, the storyteller should begin to observe and understand the listeners' perspectives of how the world works and what values and beliefs are foundational to them. Use intentional and focused listening to discover the needs, questions, and as much information as possible to understand how their society created their understanding of how the world works. For example, if their worldview includes sacrificial practices, the storyteller needs to know the expectations from the listeners' beliefs that make the sacrifice effective for them.

Identifying the story's misconception(s) is a different objective than passing along information. There are different questions to explore in the biblical story such as:

- What misconceptions are present?
- Which character or characters revealed a misconception in the story?
- Was there a false concept of God, people, sin, authority, honor, shame, fear, power, purity revealed?
- Is the misconception a faulty aspiration of the person or culture, or is the aspiration appropriate but faulty in how it seeks fulfillment or satisfaction? Does the motivation or the methodology reveal the misconception? Is there a challenge or accusation of the aspiration whereas or the need to share "a better way."
- What was the context in which the misconception was revealed?
- How did the misconception develop in the person or the culture?
- Was the misconception directly approached, challenged, or corrected in the story?
- Is the misconception a symptom of a much deeper fundamental flaw?
- What contemporary comments or questions would reveal the presence of the misconception today?

Clearly identifying the misconception(s) exposes the critical turning point in the story as the character decides to adopt, change, or reject the biblical worldview, which then guides the storyteller how to ensure those parts are emphasized more carefully. That critical point of the story affects

The Process of Creating Story Lessons

how you craft the story; don't let it be lost. When the storyteller can define the point of the story clearly and knows where the crisis moment of decision happens, it becomes easier to identify where the supporting main points of the story are located.

Try to discipline yourself to stay longer than you think necessary to brainstorm all the potential misconceptions the story might include either directly or indirectly. It is the hardest step to work through but will produce the greatest benefit and impact on how you craft the story and consider your questions later on. Don't be in a rush to get through this step; linger awhile.

Because we all tend to teach as we've been taught, we also tend to tell a story as we heard it, being influenced by the affect it had on us. But it had that impact on us in *our* own world; it might not be as relevant to another's world. So, don't retell the story from your perspective; that's how a story becomes stale. Have others learn to tell the story from *their* perspective to *their* worldview.

After considering the results of your questioning about the misconceptions, continue preparing for the story by asking, "Why would I tell *this* story at *this* time for *these* people?" That will encourage your thinking of the story from a fresh, new perspective and encourage evaluating the listeners' context or worldview, which may lead toward a new purpose. The biblical story isn't preserved in Scripture as only a historical record, but ". . . for teaching, for reproof, for correction, for training in righteousness" (2 Tim 3:16). What is it that needs to be corrected in your listeners through understanding this story?

An inability to describe the misconception with clarity may indicate that the kingdom concept of the story may be unclear in your own mind. The most critical step toward changing a misconception or worldview is to express the contrast between the current misconception and the proposed, kingdom understanding. You should be able to write or speak the misconception and the gospel's response to the misconception to another briefly with identification of the key issue. Don't assume you can communicate the misconception by simply saying it in your mind; speak it out loud. Tell another to make certain you can express it clearly. As Professor Howard Hendricks often warned in his seminary courses, "A mist in the pulpit is a fog in the pew." If you cannot speak it clearly, it will not be clear to the listener.

Part 1 : Crafting Biblical Storytelling

The same story can be crafted and told to those believing very different worldviews. For example, the creation story can address a Western, secular worldview that rejects a personal, creating God but also address a Muslim worldview that readily accepts God (Allah) as Creator. Misconceptions differ among each of us in part because the cultures shaping each of us are different and, consequently, the purpose of the stories that counter those false worldviews must be approached differently. Another example of the power and universality of the Word of God is that the same story in Scripture can counter any contrasting worldview—though the skill of the storyteller must be careful to include the specifics of the story that allow the story to be contextualized or interpreted to be able to destroy the false worldview.

Identify the Main Points

Identifying the misconception(s) present in the story guides the lesson crafter to identify points of the biblical story that build and move the story toward its conclusion and revealed truth that contrasts with the misconception. Sometimes, the conclusion might not arrive for pages or chapters in the Bible. Therefore, to keep a story simple, short, memorable, and easily reproducible requires excluding those verses that don't contribute toward the revelation of the truth, but also—and just as importantly—guides the crafter not to eliminate critical details necessary to help the listener recognize the biblical truth.

In the process of identifying those points, the story's contextualized structure forms. The structure keeps the storyteller on task, helping move the story toward its conclusion. Do not think of these main points as points toward forming a logical argument because putting a logical structure to the story is more characteristic of literate information processing than oral processing, which will be more fully explained in chapter 4. Rather, think of the points of the story as being the skeletal structure that builds the story. Practically, identifying the major points help the storyteller stay focused and moving forward when telling the story.

Keep the main points of the story as simple and few as possible—limit the story to three or four points. If more points can be made from the story, it would be preferable to craft another story that can stand on its own feet and perhaps reveal a supporting conclusion.

The Process of Creating Story Lessons

Identifying the main points becomes particularly helpful to those transitioning from a literate preference background to oral storying. Literate-oriented people want to memorize the story because of their commitment to specific words that embody truth. Consequently, even while telling the story, literate-preference storytellers are concentrating on the next word to say (often indicated by stumbling over words). To help in transitioning to the teaching style for oral learning–preference listeners, use a technique called "storyboarding," used by visual storytellers of books and movies. Storyboarding illustrators sketch each scene of a story as a picture. Use the main points of the story as the title for each scene and then fill in the picture with a stick figure or representation of the people or action in the story and draw a little balloon by the person to indicate those who are saying something in the story. If paper is unavailable, use any objects in your pockets or the surroundings to represent the characters or events. Then, when telling the story, the storyteller can focus on describing the picture rather than the specific words. The words will come with practice and frequent retelling and editing.

Identify the Biblical Passage

Identifying the main points helps define where the story begins and ends. That may not be as easy as it sounds. You might have a good story in mind to use for the misconception, but where the story begins and ends is not always as clear.

That's because the story's beginning and ending can "creep" a bit more if the story is part of a larger story that eventually goes beyond the point of addressing the misconception. Or the story might also conclude with a feeling that it is incomplete and needs to continue further—but that may be caused by the storyteller's familiarity with what happens next in the biblical account even though it isn't particularly relevant to the misconception being targeted.

Keep in mind the listener will likely have access only to the scriptures used in the story so the listener won't experience the same feelings of incompleteness or a desire to expand the story in either direction. The oral listener only wants to hear one simple, uncomplicated story at a time without subtexts and subplots; therefore, keep the story short, simple, and direct. Remember, the goal is to tell a story that is easily and immediately repeatable to another new listener. Resist the temptation to teach more information than is part of the story, which provides openings for the listener to ask questions later in the story discussion time that gets the discussion off the main point. There is also a temptation to slip in a salvation scripture, like being born again in John 3:3 or using John 3:16, that isn't the misconception in focus or relevant to the story itself.

Consequently, the storyteller must limit the story's information concerning the misconception addressed by the story to the beginning and end verses. There might be a wonderful summary verse from another book, but that should only be used for a memory verse. The passage should be viewed as the totality of Scripture for that particular point because that's the only piece of scripture made available to the listener to pass along to another. There must be enough clues remaining in the story to provide the insight the listener requires to recognize its challenge to the listener's previous worldview. This is why—before defining the length of the passage—it is critical to identify the misconception and the main points to protect the story from overediting.

With these three components (the misconception, main points, and the biblical passage) identified and clearly stated, you are ready to begin crafting the story. You now know what points of the story are critical to include and emphasize, and what should be edited to keep the story crisp, simple, memorable, and moving forward. That's the purpose for "crafting the story." Crafting is not adding or subtracting from the story, for the story is scripture and not to be changed. Rather, it is how best to deliver the story so it is understood and incorporated indigenously and repeated powerfully.

Craft the Story

"Crafting the story" refers to the editing process that defines the why, what, and how of including and excluding details of the story when retelling it with no loss or manipulation of its message. Storytelling is not scripture memory; it is not intended to be the recitation of scripture for that would be burdensome to new converts and become an obstacle to sharing the story with their friends. There is a spontaneity to oral speaking that provides an orderly arrangement of simple clauses to tell a story in chronological order. Contrastingly, written communication often goes through a process of logical grammatical relationships that becomes rather complex and polished. That's why reading from written materials is never as fresh as spontaneous speakers; we simply don't speak as we write.

The Process of Creating Story Lessons

For people, such as myself, who hold a high respect and love for the inerrancy and authority of Scripture and are conscious of the biblical warnings against subtracting or adding to Scripture, it is difficult to reduce the biblical narrative to an easily transferable story. But I remind myself that Scripture is Scripture and a story is an oral telling of Scripture for a particular God-honoring purpose in a simple style that encourages discussion. A small child retelling the story of Daniel in the lion's den is never challenged that he or she had altered Scripture. It's simply telling a story, after all!

The Scriptures encourage us to use stories to learn and grow: "For whatever was written in earlier times was written for our instruction, so that through perseverance and the encouragement of the Scriptures we might have hope" (Rom 15:4). What were written for us were the stories of hope . . . and lessons that are "profitable for teaching, for reproof, for correction, for training in righteousness so that the man of God may be adequate, equipped for every good work" (2 Tim 3:16). The value of stories to define or change us is more broadly applied than through Scriptures alone; in fact, neuroscience tells us thinking in story is hardwired in our brain.

The Structure of Story

Stories are how we make sense of an otherwise overwhelming world around us. Lisa Cron's perspective, informed by brain science, identifies story as being used by the brain for survival.

> The brain constantly seeks meaning from all the input thrown at it, yanks out what's important for our survival on a need-to-know basis, and tells us a story about it, based on what it knows of our past experience with it, how we feel about it, and how it might affect us. Rather than recording everything on a first come, first served basis, our brain casts us as "the protagonist" and then edits our experience with cinema-like precision, creating logical interrelations, mapping connections between memories, ideas, and events for future reference.
>
> Story is the language of experience, whether it's ours, someone else's, or that of fictional characters.[1]

From a biblical perspective, the story usually focuses on the historical biblical character's experience under the sovereignty of God. The events

---

1. Cron, *Wired for Story*, Kindle 179–84.

and actions are recorded in story format and analyzed according to typical story analysis that aligns with Scripture's objectives to change our lives.

> "What happens" is the plot. "Someone" is the protagonist. The "goal" is what's known as the story question. And "how he or she changes" is what the story itself is actually about. As counterintuitive as it may sound, a story is not about the plot or even what happens in it. Stories are about how we, rather than the world around us, change. They grab us only when they allow us to experience how it would feel to navigate the plot . . . What does your protagonist have to confront in order to solve the problem . . . ? And that problem is what the reader is going to be hunting for from the get-go, because it's going to define everything that happens from the first sentence on . . . So for a story to grab us, not only must something be happening, but also there must be a consequence we can anticipate.[2]

Cron concludes we love stories because they are our self-defense as we hear our problem described and explained. We can recognize it and identify with the story's protagonist to learn how he or she resolves the problem, which gives us (as the listener) a safe way of how to meet our own challenge safely. In other words, good stories help us learn from the mistakes—or victories—of others.

Cron sees the basic construction of a story as the need for the reader or listener to identify with the primary character, describe a threatening crisis besetting the character, and how that character—or the divine intervention of God—meets the challenge. This becomes our example to teach us how to successfully navigate our own situations.

Stories can take the form of myths and fables that provide examples of goodness and values. Such moral lessons are invaluable as they shape decisions both good and evil. But there is something special and powerful when learning from real events. The details found in biblical stories—such as locations and contexts that allow for validating the events to later generations—are not included in fables and myths born of fantasy. Moreover, the Bible is brutal in its exposure of both the strength and the weaknesses of its heroic prophets, priests and kings. Retelling biblical stories connects readers and listeners to biblical characters in similar situations and reveals the consequences of their actions or decisions—both favorable and

---

2. Cron, *Wired for Story*, Kindle 226–54.

The Process of Creating Story Lessons

unfavorable—with whom they can identify and provide a model for their own responses.

Following the structure of the biblical story, and having identified the biblical passage(s), the next step is to determine if the story is short, a compilation of a few stories to form a theme, or a compilation of individual verses formed into a single lesson that is not a single lesson—such as the creation of angels, which has no specific story to reproduce.

Walsh wrote an excellent descriptive list of fourteen steps to create a story. I particularly appreciate the qualities required for his selection of the story:

> I look for two—and only two—qualities: Does the story resonate with me? I want my audience to see that I am excited about the story. I can't do this if I don't like it. Besides, once I have developed the story, I may end up telling it many times. It is important that I like the story. Do I like the ending? For me, a good ending is a nonnegotiable element. I can adapt the rest of the story to fit the occasion, but good endings are hard to find.[3]

Obviously, the storyteller cannot edit the ending of a biblical story to fit into Walsh's or another writer's concept of what might constitute "a good ending." Biblically, a "good ending" is not always a "happy ending." But the story's *lesson* is good, even if perhaps in the context of a tragic story ending. It accomplishes its purpose as Scripture "for doctrine, correction, reproof, and instruction in righteousness" (2 Tim 3:16), and offers the listener hope through God.

The crafting of the story reflects skill. There are several elements to a story that make it compelling and interesting: the main points that form the structure of the story; good, insightful character development; the right kinds and amount of detail that make the story come alive; and, whenever possible, conversations. Listeners like conversations within a story because it makes them think they're hearing private information being passed from one character to another. All these good story devices provide mile markers to the story that keep the flow or the journey moving forward. The story needs to be told without word-for-word memorization to keep it natural while retaining the critical points of content. Walsh, however, points to two places in a story that should be memorized:

---

3. Walsh, *Art of Storytelling*, 27.

However, there are two parts of a story where the storyteller should not ramble: the first few sentences and the last few sentences. These should occupy a huge amount of your preparation time. Once you have crafted those beginning and ending sentences, memorize them! Know exactly what your first and last words will be before you stand in front of an audience.[4]

The process of crafting the story begins with reading or, preferably, hearing as many versions and paraphrases of the story as possible. After completing that step, do not look at a written text of the story again because it will influence the tone of the story and reflect more of a recitation instead of the fresh appeal of an oral story. Digitally record the storytelling or, preferably, begin telling the story to another. Were all the main points included? Was there enough critical content remaining for the listener to discover perspectives contrary to his or her existing misconceptions? The reason the story was selected was because there were clues within the story to counteract existing faulty beliefs, but it is possible to edit the story parts where the clues were present unintentionally. In other words, don't overedit the story so the clues are lost or covered up. The listener must still be able to discover the critical clues in the story that will influence the listener's change in perspective.

And most critically, was the story true to the scripture? This last critical step should be done by another person who can compare the story to the written text so the storyteller does not read the written text itself again. The story must maintain its faithfulness to the Scriptures. Therefore, make as many changes as necessary to the story before rerecording it or retelling it again. When comfortable with the story, memorize the first and ending lines, as Walsh suggests.

Cru's "StoryRunners" oral ministry initiative uses four evaluative criteria that must be met for each story: it must be biblically accurate, orally reproducible, naturally told, and appropriate to the culture. These four criteria should be applied to every story developed.

Developing Questions

John Dear lists a total of 307 questions that Jesus asked others and 183 questions that others asked Jesus —of which Jesus directly answered only three. What do those statistics reveal about Jesus' concerns? Jesus, as the

---

4. Walsh, *Art of Storytelling*, 51

master teacher, was not interested in using questions as an excuse to deliver more information, but to use the questions to prompt personal thinking and reflection. Such questions do need not be complex to be powerful tools. For example,

> The first question Jesus asks does not address our sins, failures, or infidelity. It is not accusatory or hostile. Rather, it is a question rooted in compassion and love, calling upon our deepest desires, the best within us. It is a question full of hope. "What are you looking for?
>
> ... Jesus' persistent questioning shows how compassionate he is. He does not hit us over the head with answers that we cannot comprehend...
>
> ... The most frequently asked question in all four Gospels is perhaps the most beautiful: "What do you want me to do for you?"[5]

The same attitude of Jesus should also be our attitude as we form the questions to ask the listener—to offer compassion and love rather than defense of our beliefs to defeat an "opponent of the cross."

The use of questions is culturally influenced because it determines how we process or learn new information. Such learning preferences that describe how people prefer to acquire, store, and remember information can be grouped into two categories: literate or oral. Literate describes those who prefer to learn based upon print text, whereas oral describes those whose learning preference is anything other than text. That's right; one category only has one learning process and the other category is everything else. These learning preferences, which will be more fully described in chapter 3, generate very significant differences in how a person prefers to learn. How a person responds to questions highlight their differences. For example, among literate learners the response to a story is often, "So what's the point?" before tearing the story apart to interpret its intention or purpose. Literate learners expect to receive conclusions to points made that are already concluded and recorded in print. But for oral learners, *the story itself* is the point! In other words, literate learners usually prefer to be told the principles first and listen to the story as an illustration of how the principles work, whereas oral learners prefer to hear the story first and then discover the principles for themselves. Oral learners don't like to tear the story apart because it would lose its quality of "storyness." Instead, they

---

5. Dear, *Questions of Jesus*, Kindle 155, 134.

want to discover how the story will provide wisdom that they can apply to their life or situation.

The literate storyteller tends to use directed, specific questions that might cross the line from letting the story speak for itself to hijacking the story's intent by defining and forcing the intended point too narrowly, quickly, and directly. Arriving at the point of the story remains the objective for hearing the story and questions are a tool to get to that point using the "approved" word choices for the answer. But proceeding too quickly and directly may damage the discovery and information processes preferred by the oral listener. Oral learners, however, are quite content hearing a story retold several times to allow them the joy of unfolding the meaning of the story through discovery and reflection. Consequently, the storyteller should remain quiet and permit the listeners' pace to process the information internally, often encouraged by the storyteller's open questions.

If the storyteller expects "the right answer" and keeps questioning until the listener gives "the right answer," it may result in debate instead of dialogue. Allowing time for dialogue enables the listener to develop ownership of what was self-discovered, which results in motivation to pass along the story to others. Questions should be open-ended with more options to discuss and evaluate. The questions, like the main points, must be short, simple, memorable, and few. Remember that our goal is to have the listener repeat the story to another, but the goal of the story's lesson includes using questions for the new listener. The questions don't need to be learned word for word, but familiarity with them should help bring the questions to mind to ask in a style that is natural and fits the tone and progress of the story.

One of the surest ways to slow or stop discussion is to offer a question that could be answered by a simple yes or no, an obvious answer requiring no thoughtfulness, or an unimportant short response. Good questions should prompt personal reflection and encourage developing other questions and raising new implications for additional thought.

Gregory Koukl describes using questions from a tactical perspective when engaged in evangelism in his book *Tactics: A Game Plan for Discussing your Christian Convictions*. Koukl writes,

> This is the value of using a tactical approach: staying in the driver's seat in conversations so you can productively direct the discussion, exposing faulty thinking and suggesting more fruitful alternatives along the way.[6]

---

6. Koukl, *Tactics*, 24.

The Process of Creating Story Lessons

Notice that Koukl's questioning tactics differ slightly from using questions to assist the listener's discovery of the story's biblical principles that conflict with the listener's worldview. Using questions is a good choice when the storyteller doesn't want to remain in the driver's seat and allows the listener to drive the discussion—but with friendly guidance through the promptings of appropriate questions. Listening carefully to the listeners' musings can provide great insight to the listener's worldview and mental processing, which is invaluable for further discussion. The storyteller is also modeling respect to the listeners by allowing their opinions to be heard—a respect that will often be returned.

The well-prepared storyteller should not only prepare for the story, but also for the questions. Developing good questions requires time, skill, a lot of persistence, and hard work. In addition to causing the listener to pause and consider new information, they must also be simple, easy to remember, and even easy to ask. The purpose of the questions is to move the conversation through the main points of the story.

There are four kinds of questions to keep any discussion moving forward: leading, guiding, summary and application questions. Leading questions introduce the subject and can set the direction of the conversation. Guiding questions are those that can readjust the questions to refine or redirect the discussion. Summary questions give opportunity to the listener to resolve the topics discussed to help give a conclusion to the discussion. And, of course, application questions ask the person to take a moment to determine what they need to do or think about next as a result of the discussion.

It's critical to refine and shape each question for your purpose. You may believe you thought of a wonderful, insightful question—until you try answering it verbally to yourself. Though the question might have seemed wonderful when unspoken in your mind, when verbalizing the question and answer aloud, you may discover the word choices don't communicate the concept in your mind well. Always test yourself by asking and answering the question aloud to yourself before asking the question to your listeners.

A question that impacts the listener—that causes the listener to be quiet for a moment and seriously and thoughtfully reflect on it before answering—is the question that the listener will most likely ask another friend when retelling the story. The question will more likely be asked if there is a connection between the storyteller and the listener over the same issues and concerns. The third-generation listener can always tell if the second-generation storyteller asked the question as part of someone else's lesson

Part 1 : Crafting Biblical Storytelling

curriculum or because the person was genuinely interested in their own personal thoughts about the lesson.

Cultural processes and values should be considered when asking questions. Some cultures respect the holiness of sacred stories, including the Bible, to the degree that questions and discussions of the sacred text would be sacrilegious. A possible solution would be to discuss issues that appear in the story beforehand as a separate discussion before telling the story, after which public discussion might be culturally disallowed. Other cultures that honor older people might not ask any questions until the oldest person responded and answered for the group. There are Asian cultures for which questions won't be asked unless the answer is already known, and there are tribal communities who are not required to answer questions truthfully unless they are sitting under the village's "truth tree." This is so the person is not shamed by exposing his or her own ignorance, or careful not to reflect on the storyteller's lack of ability to teach the story well so that questions remain.

Initially, the best way to begin questioning would be to follow the lead of the listeners. If no questions are asked or discussion made, do not force the issue. Instead, be prepared with questions but seek the leading of the Holy Spirit about how and when to use them. Do not be concerned if questions and dialogue are delayed until the listeners have had time to reflect about something, or because they want to talk to other listeners without the presence of the storyteller to confirm or question their own conclusions. The questions may not come until the next day! Story-specific questions fit the goal of addressing misconceptions.

The difficulty with story-specific questions is that they must also be remembered and passed along with the story to the next generation. "StoryRunners," the orality initiative of Campus Crusade, avoids using story-specific questions and, instead, relies upon four general questions after telling any bible story:

- What did you like about the story?
- What didn't you like about the story?
- What did you learn about man?
- What did you learn about God?

At the risk of being too general and perhaps missing the potential of exposing misconceptions, these questions are very simple to memorize,

The Process of Creating Story Lessons

easy to pass along, and capable of opening discussions that can be directed by anyone in the group. They are simple enough for someone who only heard the story one time to be able to ask them to others. To get the listeners involved in the story is a significant achievement and to be celebrated. However, it is also a good thing if there are questions prepared that could subtly direct the discussion toward the story's intended purpose. The primary goal is to have others able to retell the story and lead the discussion to others.

Jackson Atkins, president of Discipleship Multiplication International and an experienced teacher of oral strategies, suggests using questions for each main point or movement in the story.

> The storyteller asks, "In this section, what can I learn spiritually about the characters from what they are saying or doing? Did any of the characters make a choice and if they did what other choices could they have made? In this section, do I see any results from their choices, and was anyone impacted? Finally, where and how is God working in this circumstance? . . . After helping the hearers discover the truths, the storyteller helps them apply the truths through a series of application questions. These questions include "Today, does this still happen? In what ways does this still happen? Has this ever happened to you or someone you know? Will you share your experience? What in this story might help you if this happened to you in the future?"[7]

Questions encourage the listener to apply the information reflected in the story to the next step: learning to recognize the relevance of the story to his or her own worldview and determine if the character's response to the issue or concern produces a more favorable response and benefit than the listener would otherwise expect.

Selecting Scripture Memory Verses

The Word of God is neither a charm nor a compilation of magical incantations. But empowered by the Holy Spirit, the Word of God "is living and active and sharper than any two-edged sword, and piercing as far as the division of soul and spirit, of both joints and marrow, and able to judge the thoughts and intentions of the heart" (Heb 4:12). Implanting the Word

---

7. Atkins, "Multiplyinig Disciples in an Oral Context," in Chiang and Lovejoy, eds., *Beyond Literate Western Models*, 80–81.

of God into the mind of the listener allows the Holy Spirit to continue his work in the life of the listener.

Therefore, if possible and appropriate, suggest a verse that summarizes the lesson of the story for the listener. That verse can either be from either the story itself or from another portion of Scripture; it doesn't matter to the Holy Spirit because either scripture is sourced in him! However, select a verse that's short and easily memorable. But remember, depending on the cultural background of your listener, it may be important to explain that Scripture is not a magical spell; it is God's Word that must be used for the reason it was intended to be used, as explained in 2 Timothy 3:16.

Selecting the "Hook Question"

The seventh and final step to the lesson is to create a "hook" question. This is an unanswered question to leave with the listener at the conclusion of the lesson. This is that question that the person can't get out of his or her mind until the next lesson finally arrives. But, like a fish on a hook, it keeps the listener engaged in the story during the coming days or weeks. The objective is to cause the listener to personalize the lesson and remain sensitive to the lesson while continuing to experience life but, hopefully, with a sensitivity to the new perspective. Implanting an idea that serves as a persistent annoyance that needs to be resolved, it is an open-ended question that forces self-reflection. Another way of thinking about the hook question is that it is a tool the Holy Spirit can use to continue teaching when the storyteller isn't around.

Chapter Summary

A story lesson is developed from a biblical story. The story is selected because it illustrates a contrast between a biblical worldview and a faulty worldview (a misconception) held by the listener. The description of the misconception becomes the focused purpose of the lesson and identifies the beginning and end of the story. The focus upon the misconception also clarifies the main points of the story's movement and assists the story crafter to edit the story so it remains truthful but is simple, short, memorable, and easily repeated. Questions are developed to engage the listener's reflections about the story. The dialogue between the storyteller and the listener should provide new insights and perspectives exposing the contrast of the

The Process of Creating Story Lessons

biblical worldview to what had been personally believed. When possible, a suggested summary verse should be offered for memorization followed by an unanswered hook question to keep the listener thinking about personal beliefs or practices concerning the story. This story-crafting process should be consistently used so it can be passed along to others.

Chapter 2

Creating Story Lesson Sets

THE FOUNDATIONAL ATTRACTION FOR any story is the ability of the author or storyteller to draw the listener into the story by identifying himself or herself with a story's character. The stronger the identification and connection to a character, the more the listener will sense personal relevance to the story. The stories and parables that Jesus told always pulled the listener into the story by describing the characters and context so well that people finally came to realize that Jesus was talking about them more than just telling a story.

It is precisely this impact of identification with the story that J. O. Terry, a missionary and contemporary pioneer in oral storytelling, discovered when crafting topical stories that had become immediately relevant to Muslim women. Terry noticed their identification with stories about women treated wrongly by their husbands or who faced the issue of barrenness, which was often interpreted as God's judgment against them. To hear the truth that God answered those needs and defended these women was impactful and they wanted to hear more stories about this God.

Terry not only recognized the identification of Muslim women to the stories that kept them engaged, but also how, through discussion, they contributed insights into the story that otherwise would be overlooked by the storyteller. In particular, Terry discovered the presence of cultural values and the expression of those values in the biblical story that provided additional, strengthening points of connection.

> In the story "A Bride for Isaac" (Genesis 24), Abraham's servant gave Rebekah gold earrings and a nose ring after she watered his camels. Then, when it was time for the servant to depart, he asked

Creating Story Lesson Sets

if Rebekah would go with him and the family answered, "ask her." Finally, as the servant and Rebekah neared Isaac's place, she asked, "Who is that man standing there?" When the servant responded that it was his master, Rebekah covered her face with her veil. The women really loved that as it signified she was a modest woman.[1]

Moses, as the author of Genesis, did not intend the purpose of the story to be about modest practices of women but about God's plan to provide a wife for Isaac. Yet it was the modesty that gave credibility and honor to the story and perhaps an insight into the character of a person whom God chooses to honor. These insights are best revealed through discussion as a method to discover what cultural practices or personal needs can be discovered if listening to others describe what they discovered by listening to the story. Consider Terry's other observations:

> In the Ruth story, when Ruth covered herself with the corner of Boaz' robe, the women immediately knew what that meant. In the Hannah story, the fact that Hannah was barren but that her husband still loved and favored her was powerful. Then, when God answered Hannah's prayer with a son, Samuel, and later other children, this was amazing to the women. I could go on with many other interesting illustrations of things I learned from those women.[2]

But, as valuable as these cultural identifications with the women of the Bible may be, the purpose of the stories is to reveal the gospel. Terry reported the women loved the stories of Jesus and his kindness and understanding toward women in need, but the theological issue of sin—particularly forgiveness from sin—was too much of a jump from their Muslim worldview to grasp the Christian promise of forgiveness.

> The stories of the Samaritan woman at the well, the woman taken in adultery, the widow of Nain who had lost her husband and her only son (her guardians), the widow who gave the mite at the treasury, the woman who wept at the feet of Jesus—in all these, even when there was forgiveness of sin, it was the acceptance by Jesus that stood out. Jesus did not turn the women away, but helped them in their time of need.
>
> Well, I missed fully understanding this in the Bible story set (God and Woman) that I prepared for Muslim women. The

1. Personal correspondence with the author, June 22, 2015.
2. Personal correspondence with the author, June 22, 2015.

women loved the stories of Jesus but did not respond as expected to the invitation at the end of the stories. After struggling with this I realized that I had not touched in a reinforced manner on several key issues: one is that the women in that culture believed like the men that God (Allah) was distant and unapproachable. They needed to see Allah as caring and reaching out to the women more strongly.

So, in a second set of stories, I narrowed the list of worldview issues that informed the story set to deal more openly with God's "acceptance" of women and His purpose for them in creation. I touched more on the relationship with God. This story set was more intensely evangelistic and had fewer stories. The women responded to a God who could intervene in their daily needs and provide for them. I learned this was important because of the responsibility that the women carried in the Muslim family. Rather than giving an invitation to believe on Jesus as Savior, the women responded best to turning to Jesus as a God who loved and helped women. God helped the women in their "neediness." The idea of salvation and paradise by and by was lost on most. But a provident access to a God and Jesus who cared and helped each day was a real decision maker. (This set is Heaven Is for Women.) While this on the surface appears theologically shallow, I began to see how this opened the women's hearts to the Holy Spirit. I was learning that the women were far more spiritually aware and sensitive than the men.[3]

Of course, many other Muslim women did not want to express any interest in biblical stories. Terry found stories within his host culture how women released their frustrations and anxieties after personal suffering and mishaps and related to those experiences through his "Grief Stories." One of those stories centered on Mary's suffering as a woman and the mother of Jesus with the other women who witnessed Jesus' crucifixion and continued their collective pain to their joy of the resurrection. These are stories best simply told, allowing for the power of the emotions as the listeners identify with the pain. Questions would eventually emerge that led to more explanations about Jesus.

Terry was justifiably concerned that the women still responded with traditional and culturally acceptable ways of handling their frustrations, such as taking offerings to a dead holy man's tomb and beseeching spirits to ask for help. So Terry developed another series of biblical stories that

3. Personal correspondence with the author, June 22, 2015.

CREATING STORY LESSON SETS

told how women turned to Jesus for help, such as the woman with the issue of blood or the woman who wept at the feet of Jesus. Jesus' compassionate response and his support proved to be powerful proofs of Jesus' faithfulness in helping each woman.

Terry grouped these stories together, producing a menu of options: "God and Woman," "Heaven Is for Women," "Grief Stories," and "Ebenezer Stories"—each one with several stories to fit the situation. Though the original intent of the author might be different for each story, they were all similar in providing applications that were windows into God's character and care for the distinctive challenges faced by women—women apart from the grace and love of God. Consider all the women prominently recorded in these menus: Rebekah, Ruth, Hannah and the unnamed Samaritan woman, the adulterous woman, the widow at Nain, the widow and her mite, the woman who wept at Jesus' feet, Mary at the cross, and the woman with the issue of blood.

Another storyteller developer grouped his menu of 49 stories equally into seven groups or story sets. The story sets were arranged according to the "Four Fields" illustration created by Ying Kai and published in his book, "T4T" co-authored with Steve Smith. These groups are titled *Vision, Entry, Gospel, Disciple, Church, Leader, and Movement*. The seven purposes with the story selection for each of the seven groups is available at www.noplaceleft.net. The developer designed very simple icons to represent each story. There is no presentation order of the seven stories within each group, so the teacher offers the listener his or her choice to select one of the seven icons to hear the story—creating a sense of both control and inquiry in the listener. The teacher, however, has control over which group is the most appropriate for the listener and only offers the selection within his or her selected group.

Cru's "StoryRunners" storying ministry uses a chronological arrangement of stories rather than the topical menus described above. StoryRunners crafted forty-two stories using ten from the Old Testament, nineteen from the gospels, and thirteen from the Book of Acts. All these stories are available for listening on their website, www.storyrunners.org. These stories are translated and left with local people to initiate new spiritual generations of believers.

Storying T4T (S-T4T) is another storying initiative that presents its menu of stories as "story sets." The "Initial 21 Set" comprise twenty-one stories from creation to the return of Christ. The "Acts Set" are stories covering

PART 1 : CRAFTING BIBLICAL STORYTELLING

the first half of Acts to discover what makes a reproducing church. The third, "Epistles Set," comprises ten stories on the theme of becoming a new creation in Christ. These lessons, as zip files, are available to download at no cost at www.st4t.org.

John Walsh offers two websites containing stories he developed: www.bibletelling.org and www.btstories.com. These websites also include videos of his narrations for modeling how to tell stories.

James and Carla Bowman, a veteran missionary couple, began exploring the development of oral storying while in Mexico in the early 1980s. After thirty years of practice and refinement, they established an international training organization, Scriptures in Use (www.scripturesinuse.org). Their website also includes a number of stories that provide good examples for learning skills and practical application among unreached oral cultures. Carla Bowman also developed lessons for use among women with remarkable success:

> In 2005 and 2006, first encouraged by my visionary husband, I wrote a course for oral learners featuring over one hundred and twenty women's stories of the Bible to reach and disciple women. We had already been using a women's story collection since 1999 but this new workshop went far beyond that. Thematic collections were based on worldview and the unique needs and issues of women. As I worked on the thematic collections, I became convinced that God had intended to encourage and comfort his daughters throughout the millennia by including stories in his word that addressed needs, suffering, and concerns specific to them. These were changeless, timeless topics that spanned the centuries, crossing cultures and geography. The collections of stories were seen through women's eyes, beginning with creation and Eve's role in the first sin. In the Old Testament, women characters included judges, widows, queens, prophet's wives, prophetesses, and fortunetellers. In the New Testament were stories of women who followed Jesus, were healed and forgiven by Him, who sat at his feet, and served Him. There were stories revealing every human condition, every strength and weakness in the character of women. There were faithful, wise, strong, rich, poor, treacherous, evil, and skeptical women. There were models of good and bad behavior for those of oral cultures who learn best through example rather than through abstract lecture or sermons. There were situations, problems, and needs that all women from all walks of life experience. Worldview and false religion were addressed in powerful

ways. There were narratives to convict us of sin and bring hope and comfort.[4]

It makes sense to select and organize the stories and the lessons of the Bible into groups. But a decision must be made about grouping—whether it be according to the grand story of the Bible from Genesis to the gospels and beyond (often referred to as "chronological biblical storying," or CBS), grouped according to the listeners' needs, or grouped as the life of Christ. The purpose of the grouping is to better target the relevance and identification of the stories to the listeners. The design objective of CBS was to provide a series of stories from Genesis to establish the context for the coming revelation of the Messiah. These two critical learning objectives—the "logical relevance" of presenting the Messiah and the "personal relevance" identifying immediate needs—must balance each other to attract and engage listeners. How can you accomplish both objectives or establish the priority of accomplishing one before the other? That issue had to be addressed by the Bowmans as they similarly recognized the need of setting the context of the Bible before the listeners were ready to hear the story of Jesus and the role of sacrifice, and yet recognized the value of telling stories that met needs.

> As important as it was to have worldview-sensitive story collections for a given location or people group, we also found the needs-based selection of stories to be very important to a narrative ministry. Many biblical stories speak to our human suffering, weaknesses, felt needs, and relationships. Touching the lives of listeners with stories that directly addressed their own concerns has a powerful influence that cannot be overstated. Dialogue after the stories provided a worker with valuable insight into their listeners' problems as well as their spiritual growth. This also influenced their choice of future stories to tell.[5]

This decision should be made by each storyteller after prayer and observation and, in all probability, experimentation. The number of stories to include in each set is going to be determined by the skill and memory of the storyteller at the beginning, but then the capacity of retaining the stories will be established by the new believers. But consideration should also be given to the time needed to review and correct the stories as a part of the constant review process.

4. Bowman, *Building Bridges to Oral Cultures*, Kindle 2507–19.
5. Bowman, *Building Bridges to Oral Cultures*, Kindle 2445–50.

Making lesson sets helps the storyteller review the available stories and link them together to reinforce the biblical worldview for the listener by presenting the same biblical perspective through a range of life experiences described through the stories. Titles for story sets provides a helpful index to memorize to bring the stories to mind when the situation is presented.

I suggest resisting the impulse to simply download available sets as they were crafted for a different culture. Rather, develop the story from within your culture to keep the words, the pacing of the story, and the story style similar to the existing stories of the culture. However, these examples are good to begin thinking through the stories themselves. Also notice that these resource stories do not offer story lessons; the lesson format suggested in the previous chapter would still need to be applied.

Chapter Summary

Selecting and developing stories that relate to the listener's situations encourages the listeners' engagement and curiosity about a biblical response. Recognizing the positive response, the storyteller should reinforce the growing biblical insight by grouping similar stories together in sets. Grouping stories also provides a benefit to the storyteller by recalling several related stories at once.

Part 2

Countering Seven Negative Influences Affecting Storying

Chapter 3

The Influence of Mismatched Teaching and Learning Preferences

CRAFTING BIBLICAL STORIES AND story lessons are enjoyable and creative projects. They are particularly rewarding when witnessing their impact as listeners gain biblical insights into themselves and their world. But there is even greater joy in understanding *why* they are effective both educationally and strategically. Without this understanding, the story crafter or storyteller has no explanation available when the story or lesson doesn't meet with its intended success.

But seven influences, identified in these next chapters, can negatively impact the fruitfulness and success of the storytelling process. Fortunately, there are educational remedies that a story crafter can apply to counteract these influences. The first negative influence is a difference between the storyteller's preference how to teach and the listener's preference how to learn.

How do you prefer to *receive* information? How do you prefer to *give* information? Some people prefer to read books, letters, and notes—the written word—for receiving and giving information. They are described as having a *literate* learning preference. Others, however, prefer to process information through art, dance, song, drama, video, architecture, or listening; in other words, the spoken word, visual impressions, or physical activities. They are described as having an *oral* learning preference.

Literacy has nothing to do with intelligence, though many wrongly associate non-literate people with ignorance. Rather, literacy reflects how a society is organized. Societies always communicate and teach their history, values, and behaviors that define them and distinguish them from other societies. But this communication function is not always accomplished through books. Societies pass along stories to be memorized and retold to the next generation or use non-text forms such as through rituals, symbols (art), dance, drama, commemorative memorials or statues, feasts or holidays, and architecture. Dr. Charles Madinger describes orality as "... simply the ways and means of communicating orally with either a preference over textuality (print) or to the exclusion of it. In purposes of mission, orality can be defined as "a complex of how oral cultures best receive, process, remember, and replicate (pass on) news, important information and truths."[1]

Learners usually use a combination of literate and oral methods to receive, process, remember, and communicate information. Therefore, it is helpful not to think of learners as either literate or oral but rather how *reliant* a person is on one process or the other. For example, a person might either have a high or a low reliance on oral processes or a high or low reliance on literate processes that form a *preference* for learning in a particular way. Though it appeared to be an unbelievable statistic when I first heard it, "At least 80% of the world cannot or will not hear and understand our message when we communicate in literate ways and means. These people function as *oral-preference learners.*"[2] These learners include two categories of oral learners:

- those who are illiterate and *cannot* read or write, and
- those whose learning *preference* is oral though they *can* read or write.

Processing information through either oral or literate methods not only produces different types of teaching but also different types of learning outcomes. Evangelizing and discipling that depends upon a literate, text-based process is an obstacle to learners with a high reliance on oral learning. This is not saying either preference is deficient or wrong—God chose to communicate through both the oral and written word. However, our teaching should match the learner's preference as it affects the person's ability to receive, process, remember, and communicate information. Literate learners will be most effective learning and passing on information for those who have high reliance on literate forms just as oral learners will be most effective learning and passing on information for those who have high reliance on oral processes. The literate process modeled to the Apostle Paul's second and then third generation will inhibit or even halt that third generation from the ability to teach oral-preference learners of the fourth

1. Madinger, "Literate's Guide to the Oral Galaxy," 15.
2. Madinger, "Literate's Guide to the Oral Galaxy," 19.

generation. Why? Because information is processed, remembered, and reproduced differently!

Oral and Literate Learners Process Information Differently

Some broad generalizations illustrate the differences along the literate- and oral-learner spectrum. Literate-preference learners favor hearing and telling a story as briefly and directly as possible. They dislike wordiness and want to arrive at the point of the story as quickly as possible; indeed, the story is simply an optional "decoration" whose primary objective is to deliver its "point." The story itself is often unnecessary if the relevant principles are presented in an outline with bullet points. They want the *words* to do the work to explain and get the learner to recognize the point as quickly as possible.

Contrastingly, oral-preference learners believe the story itself is the point. They are not frustrated at all hearing the same story repeated over and over because they enjoy identifying principles within the story on their own, picking up new observations here and there along the story's path. Instead of depending on the words to do the work, they want to interpret the truths within the story for themselves. Accordingly, they prefer to think *around* a story's context and enjoy the trip of listening to the story before arriving at personal conclusions. Generally, oral learners could listen to a story without being told the purpose or lesson over and over again.

However, most pastoral training has been very dependent upon the written word—a literate mindset. Certainly, there is dependence on the written Scriptures and grammatical analysis of each word, sentence, and teaching based upon a logical, point-by-point explanation of each proposition. Generally, we all teach as we've been taught. If you were taught using literate processes, you saw and experienced a process that was either comfortable for or at least accommodated by you and dependent on your written notes to teach. But how effectively would you be able to adapt to a different style—an oral style? How influential has your mentor been to your teaching style?

I have always tried to imitate my teachers because I personally experienced the results of their teaching in my own life and felt a strong sense of loyalty to them. I knew their teaching deeply affected me. So now I have a literate preference in receiving, processing, remembering, and teaching information reinforced by six years of post-graduate schooling (I'm still in recovery). How well could I trust a different model to teach new information? For spiritual generations to continue, we need the ability to teach in a way that enables new believers to reproduce what they learn in a process most natural to them and to their personal network of friends without forcing them to our literate model! If the model of discipleship uses a learning style uncomfortable to them, they would be less likely to imitate that style to their friends. The teaching style must be matched to the learning style or spiritual reproduction by the new believer becomes a challenge. If the challenge is not overcome, then the new believer may even feel guilt or shame because they aren't following through on the expectation to make disciples.

Oral Preference Learners Are Everywhere; Local and Foreign

Literacy levels never remain the same in a culture: these levels constantly increase or decrease. For example, even though the United States of America is rightly described as a literate society, research indicates a growing trend toward orality and oral-preference learning. Social issues such as immigration/migration or media preferences of younger generations influence the trend toward oral-preference learners. In oral societies, the glue that holds everything together are stories—stories that ensure the values, beliefs, and heritage are passed along from one generation to the next.

The remarkable growth in the audiobook industry is another indication of the shift from literate to oral preference: "Audiobooks are the fastest-growing format in the book business today. Sales in the U.S. and Canada jumped 21% in 2015 from the previous year, according to the Audio Publishers Association."[3] This is not simply a digital phenomenon of convenience; this represents a profound change about how information is processed that is similar to oral societies. In fact, in this digital age of Twitter, communication is limited to 280 characters. Social change has prompted a direction away from literacy toward oral learning that is confirmed by years of research.

In 2003, the National Assessment of Adult Literacy (NAAL) of the U.S. Department of Education surveyed over 19,000 adults (age 16 and over) and identified those unable to process continuous prose, which is written work that flows from one paragraph to the next without subheadings such as essays, newspaper articles, journal articles, blog posts, and research

---

3. Maloney, "Fastest-Growing Format in Publishing," July 21, 2016.

papers. Those unable to process this form of printed communication was quantified by race/ethnicity. Those below basic levels of processing prose were 13 percent of Whites, 47 percent of Blacks, 50 percent of Hispanics, 18 percent of Asian and Pacific Islanders, 32 percent of American Indian/Alaska Native, and 27 percent of multiracial persons.[4] How can we share biblical truths with them using printed resources? Consider, too, that the U.S. is viewed as a literate society; the results would be much more telling among countries that are significantly less literate!

In 2007, the National Endowment of the Arts (NEA) published "To Read or Not to Read: A Question of National Consequence." The executive summary of the report concluded that "Americans are spending less time reading, reading comprehension skills are eroding, and these declines have serious civic, social, cultural and economic implications."[5] Their ninety-nine-page research report used comparative data updated from their 2004 report and concluded that "Despite exposure to higher learning in the case of college and graduate degree-holders, then, *American adults of virtually all education levels are reading less well than in the previous decade.*"[6] What's even more alarming is that the decline between 1992 and 2003 affects all education levels. Between those years, they documented the following trend concerning reading proficiency: ". . . a 20% rate of decline for adults with graduate school experience and a 22% rate of decline for other college graduates. Vocational/trade/business school graduates also experienced a significant decline in the share of proficient readers: from 9% in 1992 to 5% in 2003."[7]

The NEA report also cited the December 2006 report, "Media Multitasking among American Youth: Prevalence, Predictors and Pairings," sponsored by the Henry J. Kaiser Family Foundation. Kaiser has been tracking multitasking as a behavior and documenting an increase in using media from 16 percent of the time in 1999 to 26 percent in 2005. The significance of the data for our purposes is the identification of ten forms of non-literate communication—such as television, music, email, instant messaging, video games, web surfing—that are preferred to accompany literate reading.[8]

The National Center for Education Statistics of the U.S. Department of Education reported that the Organization for Economic Cooperation

---

4. Kutner et al., "Literacy in Everyday Life," 17.
5. NEA, "To Read or Not to Read," 7.
6. NEA, "To Read or Not to Read," 65 (emphasis original).
7. NEA, "To Read or Not to Read," 65.
8. Foehr, *Media Multitasking Among American Youth*, 1.

and Development (OECD) established the Program for the International Assessment of Adult Competencies (PIAAC), who surveyed 24 participating countries in 2012 and nine additional countries in 2014. The report indicated that, "Compared with the U.S. average score, average scores in 7 countries were higher, in 6 countries they were lower, and in 8 countries they were not significantly different."[9]

The impact of literacy is obvious for those dependent on the Bible text and printed Christian resources. A literary analysis of the Bible reveals 75 percent of the Bible contains 550 to 1,000 stories in prose style. The wide numeric spread is not because the stories haven't been counted, but because of how the stories are interpreted. Some interpret several stories as parts of only one larger story while others count the separate but related stories individually. What is undeniable and significant is that Jesus used stories as his primary teaching delivery method, and then questioned his listeners on how they discovered the inconsistencies or principles that led them toward a kingdom worldview far different from their currently held beliefs.

Also consider the significant implications for communicating biblical stories in the world. There are about 6,500 spoken languages in the world; if dialects are counted, the number doubles to roughly 13,000! With only 2,500 of those languages having some portion of Scripture translated in their heart language, the implication is unavoidable that many people have no choice but to learn the Bible orally. There has been great progress, such as the Digital Bible Library (thedigitalbiblelibrary.org), which presently provides Bible text in 1,209 unique languages including 563 complete Bibles, 969 either Old or New Testaments, and 93 Scripture portions. Additionally, there is audio for 467 unique languages including 238 complete Bibles and 410 testaments. But compare these encouraging numbers to the target of 13,000 languages, or the access to computer and online capabilities, in addition to the learners with high orality reliance. Does God have a different strategy for those without access to his scriptural revelation?

Biblical Models Supporting Oral Teaching to Oral Learners

While camped by the Jordan River opposite the city of Jericho, Moses assembled the tribes of Israel from their tents to tell them what he just heard from God: he would not be leading them into the Promised Land. After that shocking revelation, Moses immediately affirmed Joshua as their new

9. National Center for Education Statistics, "Fast Facts: Literacy," 1.

Mismatched Teaching and Learning Preferences

leader with the promise that God would be with Joshua as God had been with him and that God would still lead them into the land. But then Moses turned to complete his writing of the Law—likely the book of Deuteronomy—as the last of the five books he wrote. Moses turned over his writings to the priests who carried the ark of the covenant and instructed the priests to assemble Israel at the Feast of Booths every seven years, where they were to read all of the Law to the nation (Deut 31:9–11).

Think of Moses as the nation's educator and not just the nation's leader. What was his curriculum design strategy? It was writing and reading—a literate learning process. For Moses, this was his default to receive, process, remember, and reproduce God's truth. It was a natural choice for Moses, who had received the finest education possible in Pharaoh's court. But that was not the learning preference of those who had been enslaved and denied access to public education for four hundred years! Moses was Israel's first author, but would the literate strategy Moses used be effective for all the people and their children to hear, learn, and fear the Lord? God evidently did not think so!

Certainly, it was God's idea to have his revelation recorded in writing. But God revealed himself through many methods, and the appropriate method must be chosen for the learner. The educators Ward, McKinney-Douglas, and Detoni summarized this principle well:

> One of the most important requirements for effective learning is compatibility of the planned experiences and the learners. Each proposed target population must be carefully studied and understood in terms of three major factors that relate to effective learning: 1) motivations, value systems, and reward systems within which learners live and work, 2) previously acquired skills, and 3) expectations about learning and the learning environment.[10]

A literate process was not suitable for unskilled and illiterate learners who had been slaves for over four hundred years. Moses' consideration of their inability to read was to have all the books read to them by literate Levitical priests. Paul's strategy of 2 Timothy 2:2 was to identify faithful men (a character trait) who had the ability to teach (a skill) others also. This is a strategy of spiritual multiplication to train others who could replace the training Paul had begun. Superimpose Paul's strategy over Moses' process and it would be very different; Moses' listeners would not be able to reproduce what was read to them once every seven years. There would

---

10. Ward et al., "Effective Learning in Nonformal Modes," 34.

be no multiplication. But Deuteronomy continues and reveals God had a different curriculum design that was appropriate for the slaves' skill levels and their learning preference.

God met Moses and Joshua in the tent of meeting and revealed the future: the people would not listen to his Law and he would respond by angrily turning his face from them (Deut 31:16–18). The effects would be that Israel had no way to recognize and understand the purpose of God's discipline.

That's when God selected a different educational strategy: the non-literate, oral teaching method of song. The Lord commanded Moses to write a song to be taught from father to son for generations to come (31:19–21). Songs can be easily learned, remembered and memorized, and repeated in a style common and comfortable to their culture.

The purpose for Moses' song was for them to recall God's goodness and his warnings about their unfaithfulness to him for which they would be disciplined. Don't miss this point: God chose a non-literate educational strategy to reach the people during a time they would forget Scripture and have no interest in it. Being people of an oral culture, God selected an easily learned teaching tool available to everyone, even those who could not read what Moses had written. They would sing songs for generations and encouraged to believe and apply the lyrics. Don't slip over that phrase in the passage "for generations to come" because that's our strategic goal: produce generations. God was telling Moses what the curriculum method should be in this case. When the time came that they would be disciplined, the memorized lyrics focused their attention and reminded them of what they needed to do.

This attention to oral communication doesn't reduce the value of written Scripture. When Josiah, king of Judah, directed the repair of the temple, his high priest, Hilkiah, discovered the book of the Law. When Josiah heard the commands of God *read* to him, he recognized the level of Judah's disobedience of God, and led his nation to restoration and, after the book of the Law was read to the people the covenant was renewed (2 Kings 22:3—23:3). The choice of literate or oral communication is never a debate about comparative value or authority; it's a decision about which method seems more appropriate or effective to meet the learner's preference.

Church hymns remain educationally effective in communicating theological truths as they have for centuries past. God's choice of teaching by song remains effective among cultures where teaching by music is common. Oral educational strategies include not only songs and stories, but also art and drama. Annually celebrating the Passover according to detailed instructions (Exod 12:14–28), putting the twelve stones into the river Jordan as a memorial to the Jews crossing the river on dry ground (Josh 4:1–7) or participating in feasts and festivals all contain an educational purpose. Even the architecture requirements for the tabernacle and temple were designed to communicate spiritual truths in non-literate ways for oral-preference learners who process information differently than through written text.

"God, after he spoke long ago to the fathers in the prophets in many portions and in many ways" (Heb 1:1) confirmed his choice of different learning activities. The Apostle Paul summarized God's purpose when he wrote, "For whatever was written in earlier times was written for our instruction, so that through perseverance and the encouragement of the Scriptures we might have hope" (Rom 15:4). Hearing the acts of God recounted in stories and through songs or other methods is always for the purpose of providing hope through understanding the faithfulness of his acts.

God instructed the collection of his works not just to be written for the archives, but to be instructive "from one generation to the next." Notice how the process of "telling" is emphasized in the following psalms using words like "declare," "words of my mouth," or "our fathers have told us."

> O God, You have taught me from my youth, and I still declare Your wondrous deeds. And even when I am old and gray, O God, do not forsake me until I declare Your strength to this generation, Your power to all who are to come. (Ps 71:17–18)

> Listen, O my people, to my instruction; incline your ears to the words of my mouth. I will open my mouth in a parable; I will utter dark sayings of old, which we have heard and known, and our fathers have told us. We will not conceal them from their children, but tell to the generation to come the praises of the Lord, and His strength and His wondrous works that He has done. For He established a testimony in Jacob and appointed a law in Israel, which He commanded our fathers that they should teach them to their children, That the generation to come might know, even the children yet to be born, that they may arise and tell them to their children. That they should put their confidence in God and not forget the works of God, but keep His commandments. (Ps 78:1–7)

> One generation shall praise Your works to another, and shall declare Your mighty acts.
> On the glorious splendor of Your majesty and on Your wonderful works, I will meditate.
> Men shall speak of the power of Your awesome acts, and I will tell of your greatness.
> They shall eagerly utter the memory of Your abundant goodness and will shout joyfully of Your righteousness. . . . They shall speak of the glory of Your kingdom and talk of Your power; to make known to the sons of men Your mighty acts and the glory of the majesty of Your kingdom. (Ps 145:4–7, 11–12)

It was through God's actions by which he revealed himself to one generation intending that those acts be told to following generations—both physical and spiritual. These stories must be told and recalled to prevent the peril of forgetfulness.

> The sons of Ephraim were archers equipped with bows, yet they turned back in the day of battle.
> They did not keep the covenant of God and refused to walk in His law.
> They forgot His deeds and His miracles that He had shown them. (Ps 78:9–10)

Asaph, the author of Psalm 78, reminded his listeners by calling attention to stories of God's actions he believed had been forgotten. The writers of Psalms 104 through 107 also wrote the actions of God, both historically and prophetically, as reminders of the people. Notice that the psalmists didn't repeat the full biblical stories, but edited and summarized the stories to fit their purposes for writing—a model for us how to tell these stories to fit an intentional purpose today.

To illustrate the power of an oral story, consider Rahab of Jericho when she first met the Israelite spies (Joshua 2). Read this story from her perspective of the impact of oral stories as Rahab said to the men:

> . . . *I know* that the Lord has given you the land and that the terror of you has fallen on us, and that all the inhabitants of the land have melted away before you. *For we have heard* how the Lord dried up the water of the Red Sea before you when you came out of Egypt, and what you did to the two kings of the Amorites who were beyond the Jordan, to Sihon and Og, whom you utterly destroyed. *When we heard it* our hearts melted and no courage remained in any man any longer because of you, for the Lord your God, He is

> God in heaven above and on earth beneath ... Now swear to me by your God, since I have dealt kindly with you that you will spare my father and mother, brothers and sisters and their families and deliver us from death. (Josh 2:9-13, emphasis added)

She twice told the spies that the information came from reports or stories her people had heard. Sihon and Og's defeats were current news that took place just across the Jordan River from Jericho; not far away and obviously significant to them. But she also reported how her people were influenced by the story of the parting of the Red Sea that happened a generation earlier who, like the Israelites, were now all deceased. It was an historical event in a distant land. How did Rahab know those stories? The spies hadn't told her! Those stories were so powerful that they didn't require Israelites to tell them; non-believing Gentiles told stories of God that led to testimonies of recognition and trust in God among other Gentiles!

The stories revealed God to Rahab. Don't minimize her response! Those two stories caused Rahab to conclude that God was all-powerful. From the stories and reports she could testify, "*I know* that the Lord has given you the land ... for the Lord your God, He is God in heaven above and on earth beneath" and concluded her only hope to escape the wrath of God was to rely on a promise from God's covenant people to include her and her family under their protection. Such is the reasoning and power of having the mighty acts of God told and retold. Rahab did her own interpretation of the events of the stories as did the other Jericho inhabitants and that was sufficient to cause them to fear God and seek his shelter. That's a lot of influence from unbelieving Gentiles telling stories!

Jesus spoke of the power of belief resulting from hearing his acts when he said, "Believe Me that I am in the Father and the Father is in Me; otherwise, believe because of the works themselves" (John 14:11). Works are not arguable events; they happen and are subject to witnesses' verifications. The parting of the Red Sea and the destruction of the Amorites were not arguable. Even as some might argue today about the historicity of those events, the reaction of the citizens of Jericho demonstrated they were convinced the events happened! Observers of the dead bodies of the enemy kingdoms provided sufficient validation. Just as many might argue about the historicity of Jesus' miracles, the evidence that thousands of those who saw and knew of his miracles provides us with sufficient verification by the early witnesses that has lasted for centuries. And that's why Jesus himself said that when his words do not result in belief, the works should be told to persuade the listener to believe.

Oral learners, whether in ancient Jericho or in contemporary cultures, process information best by hearing the stories of events and works and then discovering and acting upon their own conclusions from those stories. When they respond in belief, they have constructed their own personal testimony and conviction to share with others.

Using the word "story" often carries unfortunate misunderstandings such as "stories are written for teaching children (implied is that they were not written for adults)" or "stories are entertaining and add fictional elements to keep interesting." Some might use biblical stories as fables with a moral lesson to them but no actual history. But such misconceptions reveal a woeful lack of awareness of the powerful influence story has over culture. A Moroccan friend told me, "Moroccans write with their mouths and speak with their ears." Such is the process of how their people learn to live in their oral world.

Older generations from cultures that no longer value stories of their heritage as they had once done are often dismayed and perplexed why the new generation appears to reject the same values or fail to understand their nation's history. Members of the younger generation don't know because they weren't told the stories that established the values and behaviors of their country and so do not value those stories. The stories that ultimately define a culture's behaviors and values are passed along through story; those who do not pass their stories to the following generation do so at the peril of their culture.

Strategic Implications of Oral Storying

Stories are about people and the events in their lives with whom the listener can personally identify and, in that identification, discover principles, strategies and ideas that provide insight for their own decisions. Stories demonstrate their primary strategic value as being accessible, powerful, inviting, natural, and influential.

> Stories are the most powerful delivery tool for information; more powerful and enduring than any other art form. People love stories because life is full of adventure and we're hardwired to learn lessons from observing change in others. Life is messy, so we empathize with characters who have real-life challenges similar to the

ones we face. When we listen to a story, the chemicals in our body change, and our mind becomes transfixed. We are riveted when a character encounters a situation that involves risks and elated when he averts danger and is rewarded.[11]

Our primary strategy is to encourage and enable new converts to introduce Jesus quickly to their own relational networks using stories about God (particularly the gospel). Therefore, it is more effective and achievable to have people learn, retell, and discuss stories than to learn theological propositions that become subject to challenge, debate and potential defeat for the new believer. Without immediately sharing the stories, the potential for spiritual reproduction likely ends with that first convert. Instead, we are looking to produce and multiply storytellers who allow for shared discussion of a story rather than expecting new believers to assume an uncomfortable role for which they are not equipped.

This strategy requires the storytelling to be modeled competently—but not necessarily as a polished presentation. If a new believer is awed by the polished delivery of a storyteller, it may cause the listener to say, "Oh! I could *never* tell a story as well as that person!" That response is a failure of the goal of having the listener retell the story to the listener's personal relationships. This is not an excuse for a storyteller to be boring and confusing; that's being incompetent. But the goal is to tell a biblical story that is alive and relevant and to model for others how to tell the story to another who has never before heard a story of God's revelation. The relative contribution of being a polished speaker was minimized by Paul when he wrote,

> And when I came to you, brethren, I did not come with superiority of speech or of wisdom, proclaiming to you the testimony of God . . . and my message and my preaching were not in persuasive words of wisdom, but in demonstration of the Spirit and of power so that your faith would not rest on the wisdom of men, but on the power of God. (1 Cor 2:1, 4–5)

The power of telling biblical stories does not rest upon the greatness of the storyteller but on the greatness of the stories! That was the lesson of Rahab; it was the story and not the power of the Gentiles who told their stories. Though other oral methods such as dance art, or drama are useful, their presentations require skills usually uncommon among most of us,

---

11. Duarte, *Resonate*, Kindle 625–30.

which is why the primary emphasis is upon storytelling in this book which is available to all.

A second strategic value of oral storying is its independent freedom from printed resources. Eliminating the need for printed materials eliminates the investment expenses of time, employing translators and writers, literacy training, print production and the distribution of materials. A nonbeliever shared his observation with a colleague that, since all Christians carried books, because he was illiterate he could never be a Christian. When presenting the gospel or teaching a practice or principle of discipleship, the evangelist or discipler is never solely passing along information but simultaneously modeling how to help others learn. Not requiring printed materials provides a strategic advantage for a new believer who experienced hearing and discussing the story and then was immediately qualified to retell the story and lesson without dependence on any media or even the original storyteller! How empowering!

Security is a third strategic value of oral storying. Without storing printed materials, there is no incriminating evidence of stockpiled inventory jeopardizing a storyteller's personal security. Moreover, without holding printed materials in hand, if a storyteller discerns growing hostility and rejection by a listener, the story can be quickly ended and the conversation changed without the awkward and obvious removal of any offending material. A female colleague of mine once met with Mohammad, an inquirer from North Africa, in a public restaurant (cultural etiquette would reject a private meeting). When Mohammad entered the restaurant, he was very apprehensive that there might be a Bible in sight, which would reflect badly on him in his North African neighborhood. But the two enjoyed coffee together and Mohammad remained calm as my colleague told biblical stories even as other North Africans entered the restaurant, cast a glance to see two people drinking coffee, and ignored them. A few weeks later, he affirmed his faith in Jesus as Savior and Lord.

Nik Ripken, author of *The Insanity of God*, recounted meeting a secret gathering of about 150–170 leading pastors from among the persecuted church in China. The pastors referred to their standard three-year prison sentences as their own version of seminary enrollment. Imprisonment was so pervasive that they wouldn't trust a person with leadership of a house church who had not experienced at least one prison term.

But Ripken interviewed two pastors and became perplexed by their responses that didn't appear to indicate the maturity in the Lord that was so apparent in the other pastors. Finally, in a meeting before all the pastors, those two men stood up and told their personal stories:

> But when we were arrested, we barely knew who Jesus was! We did not know how to pray! We did not know the Bible! We did not know many songs of faith. We have to confess this to you today and beg your forgiveness. For three years in prison, we did not share our faith with one person. We hid our faith. And yet, when we came out of prison, you made us leaders just because we had been put in jail. The truth is, we failed Jesus in prison. Would you please forgive us? *You can only grow in jail what you take to jail.*[12]

Entering prison results in confiscation of personal items and, most certainly in hostile foreign lands, Bibles. What can a prisoner take past the guards into his or her cell? Only that which is hidden in the mind will be available to the believer—the stories of the Bible that continue to be orally told behind the prison walls.

Education Requirements for Teaching Stories

The strategic benefit of matching the teachers' preference to the learners' preference is that the learner will feel more comfortable imitating the model and therefore more likely to share with another. But, when crafting story lessons, there are other educational curriculum design requirements that must be met. Without satisfying those requirements, the story is only a recitation for information or entertainment. To "be able to teach others" as the Apostle Paul commanded Timothy does not demand complex understanding of biblical truth at this point. The emphasis is on reaching others and teaching truth that is easily reproducible. The following curriculum design requirements are necessary to ensure the stories are memorable and enjoyable to hear and told repeatedly.

1. The story should be simply constructed, short, and memorable so it is easily transferable to another spiritual generation, requiring no further Christian theological training or understanding to be told.
2. The story requires no additional resources, being only dependent on memory and oral telling.

---

12. Ripken, *Insanity of God*, 252, emphasis added.

PART 2 : COUNTERING NEGATIVE INFLUENCES

3. The story is appropriate for evangelism or discipleship of a new believer.

4. The story is able to be taught by new disciples within the community and not dependent upon teachers outside the community.

5. The story is not personally threatening to the listener but can cause as much conviction or change as the listener permits.

6. The story should be written with words common to the listeners, which helps the listeners to identify with the events or characters of the story and to repeat the story naturally to others.

7. Stories are united around the single idea of simplicity. Simplicity is required if we want the lesson to be easily remembered and transferable—no matter what the content or objective of the lesson is. I discovered simplicity through failure: my first lessons were so doctrinally heavy that local missionaries told me they had to study among themselves before beginning to use the lessons with others! I immediately deleted my lesson files and shredded my papers, counting the translation costs already paid as my tuition to learn this lesson, and started over.

More educational design strategies will be discussed in Part 3.

Chapter Summary

Paul explained to Timothy that spreading his teachings was dependent upon Timothy's ability to enable faithful men to teach others also—a process of reproducing spiritual generations. Though negative influences can work against spiritual generational reproduction, their influence can be blunted through curriculum design.

Evangelizing or discipling using educational methods highly reliant upon written text will not be effective for people who are highly reliant upon non-textual, oral forms of receiving, processing, remembering and communicating information. Over 80 percent of the world's population are either highly reliant upon oral methods or prefer to learn using oral methods. Oral methods are not restricted to storytelling, but also include art forms, rituals, memorials, and drama—anything that teaches without dependence on written literature.

Mismatched Teaching and Learning Preferences

Oral-preference learners process information differently than literate-preference learners, therefore requiring more than simply changing selected media. The arrangement or crafting of lessons must also be different to accommodate a different logical progression of information and a different process for interaction with the information (e.g., moving from instructive lecture to facilitating discovery through dialogue).

Examples of oral storytelling are found throughout the Scriptures, and were often used by Jesus—and the Scriptures themselves instruct on the importance of telling God's acts from generation to generation. There are also strategic advantages associated with storytelling that should be acknowledged such as safety in security, capability of a listener to pass on the story immediately, and freedom from translating, printing, and delivering materials, avoiding both time delays and expense.

To encourage and enable new believers to tell stories, the stories should be simply constructed, short, and memorable.

Chapter 4

The Influence of the Listener's Own Worldview

DESPITE BEING ACCURATELY RETOLD, stories might not always be effective and might still be misunderstood by the listener. The reason for this may come from underestimating the power of the listeners' worldview that reinterprets the story to fit their existing beliefs even as they listen to the story. How can the storyteller break through each listener's own interpretations of the story to make the biblical interpretation apparent? This challenging influence appeared when Jesus told stories.

Jesus had just finished telling a parable when his disciples asked why he taught using parables (Matt 13:10ff.). Jesus answered with three points. The first point addressed the capabilities of the listeners: those who could and those who could not know the mysteries of the kingdom of heaven was based upon God's selection. The second point addressed only those listeners who could understand the mysteries for they would continue to learn much more. The third point addressed the listeners' inability to understand their world. They saw but didn't perceive; they heard but didn't understand. Jesus quoted the prophet Isaiah from seven hundred years earlier (so this was not a new problem!) when he said, "Therefore I speak to them in parables; because while seeing they do not see, and while hearing they do not hear, nor do they understand" (Matt 13:13).

Certainly, there are unknown spiritual criteria concerning God's selection of who would understand his words and who would receive the illumination of the Holy Spirit, but let's focus on the learning process. The conclusions of the previous chapter were that oral teaching is most effective for oral preference learners and that telling stories is a significant and

The Influence of the Listener's Own Worldview

powerful application of oral learning. But in this passage, we see that some listeners couldn't understand what they were hearing or interpret the acts and miracles of Jesus as they listened or saw them firsthand! We will inevitably face the same issue when telling stories to our new generation. Why do listeners "fail to perceive or gain understanding"? The answer to that question is the second negative influence affecting spiritual reproduction: the persistent presence of currently held unbiblical worldviews.

The religious leaders of Jesus' time had established a "conceptual framework" (the term used by educational psychologists instead of the social anthropologists' term of "worldview") to describe the coming Messiah and the coming kingdom. Jesus, however, did not fulfill their descriptions of the Messiah or the kingdom so Jesus' acts, miracles, and teachings were dismissed as irrelevant or the work of the devil. They could see what Jesus was doing and hear his teaching, but only a few could escape their preconceptions and truly see, hear, and perceive to gain understanding. Once they identified and rejected those misconceptions, they could understand more about Jesus and the kingdom. But those who refused to reconsider and reject their misconceptions hardened their hearts and became even more resistant (Matt 13:10–13).

Without telling stories that reveal the contrast between a biblical perspective and the listener's misconceived perspectives, the listener will initially try to interpret the story according to their own understanding or worldview. They will redefine the words themselves to make the new ideas harmonize with their beliefs or dismiss the entire story as irrelevant because "while seeing they do not see and while hearing they do not hear, nor do they understand" (Matt 13:13). To make stories is a strategic and fruitful strategy to affect the process of change, but to understand the process requires understanding how worldviews or concepts are formed.

Worldview and Conceptual Formation

"That wasn't how it was supposed to work!"

What do you do when your plans fail? In the majority of the Western world, there is an emphasis on cause and effect. If something doesn't turn out as expected, there is a reason for it and the cause can be identified and corrected. However, in much of the world there is no such expectation for a cause; failure is attributed to fate. Regardless of our expectations of predictability, our understanding of how the world works comes from the beliefs, values, and processes adopted by the family and community of which we're members—and frequently communicated through personal anecdotes and stories.

We all want to know how the world works to ensure our health, our ability to thrive, and our potential or desire to be successful. We also need to figure out who we are—to know our ancestry and learn, if possible, about our forefathers and knowing where we fit in this world. We take our personal experiences and observations, adjust and combine them with community and family views and then alter, embellish, diminish, confirm, or reinforce our views to ensure we're as safe and successful as we can be, emotionally established, and ready to face the world.

But it's a big world out there, so how do we observe and interpret all that's in it to form a comprehensive and accurate view of the world? We must decide if the world is our friend or our enemy. Will the world permit us to succeed and thrive or must we learn how to subdue it by understanding its governing principles? What must we know to either work in harmony with the world or how to overcome it? Do we understand the cause-and-effect relationships by which our world operates or do we accept the rule of fate? Are we capable of controlling those effects or are the things that affect us—either for good or ill—directed by chance, fate, inherent laws and principles, or by such divine foreordination that our own actions and initiatives are irrelevant?

Our minds are constantly observing, interpreting, and trying to make meaning of all that surrounds us to identify the things that could be dangerous or otherwise threaten us. But there is too much information in this world to be evaluated! Our mind needs a strategy to prioritize and understand all that our senses and knowledge bring to it. And our mind has such a built-in strategy; it's called categorization.

Forming Information into Concepts

Categorizing (sorting and grouping) new information is our mind's first strategy toward interpreting all the information we need to process. We first sort new information that appears most relatable to old information we have already gathered. These new blocks of categorized information become connected as we begin to understand how they relate to each other and to other concepts. The process can be visualized as if building a wall (see Figure 1). These related concepts continue to enlarge and become our framework to explain the world around us. Some concepts join with other concepts to propose behaviors that should produce success. Other concepts suggest values that should be adopted for success. Beliefs become solidified as the information, behaviors, and values relate, reinforce, and validate each other. The process includes eliminating inconsistencies in the relationships of smaller concepts to refine conclusions that are increasingly broad, comprehensive, and foundational. These larger, controlling concepts become more defensible and eventually "proven facts" to help us interpret and understand how to thrive in our world.

FIGURE 1

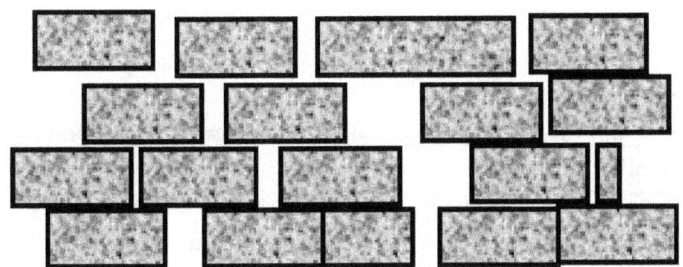

Understanding how groups and categories are formed is foundational to explain how new information fits into existing worldviews. We look for similarities between new information and existing categories already familiar to us. Information never stands alone in a vacuum. *All learning stands upon and with prior learning.* Because no one knows everything, there are always empty spaces or gaps in our conceptual structures. New information can be inserted into those gaps, but only if they agree or are similar with the concepts already believed that surround those gaps.

The theories of Jean Piaget (1896–1980), the brilliant Swiss clinical psychologist known for his work in child cognitive development, are particularly helpful here. Piaget defined the process of bringing new information into existing knowledge and perceptions as *assimilation*, and this process required *equilibration*—that is, it had to be consistent with the pre-existing knowledge. However, if new directly conflict with pre-existing concepts, other strategies are used to resolve the inconsistencies—a step Piaget called *accommodation*.

A default response to resolve or accommodate an inconsistency is to redefine the meaning of key words and mask any apparent conflict. It's the classic case of, "You might have *said* this, but I *heard* this" in order to keep the worldview consistent with itself. For example, I was a heretic about the nature of the Trinity until my fourth year of seminary! I could pass all the tests for the previous three years because I knew the right words to use for the definition, but I was defining the words to fit what I thought they were saying to conform to my current beliefs. But in my fourth year during a history of doctrine course, I finally heard a complete explanation about my heresy—called modalism—which was the first time I heard what I believed clearly defined and explained why it was heretical. Many times, theology schools do an excellent job teaching what a doctrine *is,* but fail to teach what a doctrine *is not.* It is in describing the negative misconceptions that a person is best able to identify his or her personal beliefs and relate to what is being taught. With the contrasting meaning clearly understood for the first time, I could reject my false concept of the trinity.

Sometimes, no accommodation can be made with pre-existing concepts; the new information is so foreign that it can't be grouped with anything familiar. In such situations, it often quite literally "goes in one ear and out the other" because it simply has no place to land. What cannot be resolved is often dismissed as irrelevant or untrue. Another common response is to compartmentalize the conflicting information for later times. The human mind is fully capable of holding two or more conflicting ideas at once and ignore the inconsistencies until intentionally brought together and challenged so the person is forced to recognize the inconsistency and make a decision to accept or reject the information.

Piaget called the conflict status between two (or more) competing ideas a period of *disequilibration*—an unsettling time of recognizing that an apparent misconception exists and a concept or belief must be rejected or somehow defended. But pre-existing worldviews or concepts are exceptionally persistent and not easily changed; they are naturally resistant to the discomfort of disequilibration. This is the educational explanation why Jesus spoke to them in parables . . . "because while seeing they do not see, and while hearing they do not hear, nor do they understand" (Matt 13:13). They were stuck in their own worldview about the Messiah and the kingdom and couldn't relate new information to it.

Piaget's educational theory, called *constructivism*, suggests new information is a "product of the interaction of the world and the organizing action of the person."[1] In other words, each person chooses how the

---

1. Biddell et al., *Model Building*, 1986.

The Influence of the Listener's Own Worldview

information is organized, or grouped, to make the most sense to that person. Those choices are most often influenced from personal experiences, the family, schooling, and from social conformity. Because worldviews or cognitive structures are individually constructed, only the individual can alter his or her worldview. *We are therefore incapable of changing another person's worldview.* The best we can do is get another person to discover their own inconsistency and work toward its resolution.

Because we individually categorize or sort information according to relationships that are comfortable for us, there will be a variety of category headings that are based on individual values or relationships. To appreciate how you, I, and every other person categorize differently and how that influences our teaching, I ask you to complete the following exercise. It will be best if you do this with others in your family or group, but this exercise will only be impactful if it is completed before reading the comparisons that follow.

Your assignment is to organize (group) the items listed below according to their most natural relationships. You may create as many or as few groups as you feel necessary. Include every item in a group but do not put any item in more than one group.

Cows	Grass	Angel
Birds	Whale	Virus
God	Rock	Dog
Lion	Fish	Germ
Demon	Ancestor	Bush
Man	Sand	Woman

Finally, write a title for each group identifying the common connecting reason.

Have you completed the exercise? Please complete it before reading further.

If you did this exercise as a group exercise and asked everyone to share their groupings, you likely were surprised how differently we all group common things. As an example, this exercise was given to Massai tribesmen in Africa. These tribesmen grouped man, whale, and lion together. Did you group those together? Does it seem strange to you? They grouped them together as "rulers of their domain." They grouped cows and woman together because they saw both of them as "valuable and life-giving." They grouped God, demon, ancestor, angel, virus, and germ together as "things that can kill you." And finally, they grouped birds, grass, rock, fish, sand, dog, and bush as "things that cannot talk to you."

There is nothing remarkable about these items; they are commonly known by you and the Massai. And once you heard the reasoning for the different categories, you probably thought they were reasonable—just different. But despite commonly defining the same items, the categories in which they were related and placed were uniquely defined using your own personal and cultural values and meaning. These results illustrate the constructivist theory of learning that knowledge is the product of the learner's own organization of concepts rather than that of the teacher. Appreciating this conceptual formation process and how it is individually built by the learner provides awareness of how a variety of worldviews can be developed and explain why some worldviews can be wrong (a misconception) or at least incomplete.

Adding new information into an existing worldview structure can often lead to syncretism—a mixture of truth and error that ultimately distorts the truth. To reinforce what was stated above, our minds can hold competing concepts simultaneously for long times until contradictory beliefs are placed side to side and *force* a choice by selecting one concept and rejecting the other. Unless both choices are made—to select one and reject the other—both positions are held as equally available options and our response selection is dependent on the context of the moment to choose one possible explanation or response over the other.

Becoming consistent with our concepts about the world does not happen easily. Until a concept is either rejected or chosen over other ideas, it remains vulnerable to influences and implications from other convictions, values, or practices.

The Influence of the Listener's Own Worldview

Figure 2

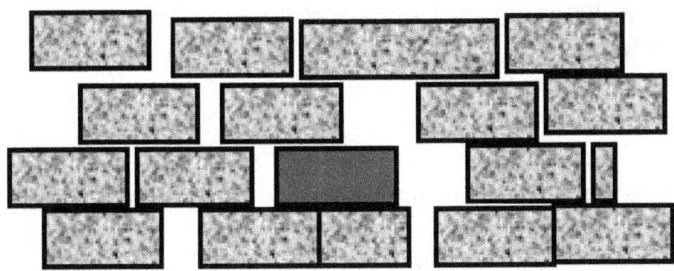

In this illustration, one block of information, represented as a solid color, is unsupported by nearby surrounding information blocks. It is more susceptible to the other influences rather than becoming the influencer. But supporting ideas can fill in other knowledge gaps until the newer ideas become defensible and preferable. This is one way to visualize progressive sanctification as a person slowly brings all the surrounding areas of life under the lordship of Jesus Christ through the power of the Holy Spirit.

Jesus used the strategy of changing listeners' categories to change their worldviews in his Sermon on the Mount in Matthew 5:21–32. He wanted them to recognize their own evaluations of fulfilling the Law were insufficient—righteousness demanded a higher commitment to the spiritual in addition to the physical. So he took their conceptual category of murder and added "anger" and "insult" to its definition. Then he took their conceptual category of adultery and added "lust" and "divorce" to the definition. He took their practice of making oaths and excluded all oaths as being evil because no one had the right to claim ownership of whatever they used as the basis for their oath. Jesus added attitudes and behaviors to their categories and the additional criteria devastated their self-righteous definitions of their pure standing before the Law. Categories matter!

Building Values into a Worldview

When do we begin forming these categories of the world around us? My good friend Jim had a long and successful career as a missionary in Africa. He described an experience entering an African village where a two-year-old boy was standing by the village water well and crying. What was unusual was that no one responded to him—not his mother, not another adult, and not the other children. No one. Jim discovered that one of the tribe's values was self-reliance to the point of not trusting others. They taught this value by carrying the infant child everywhere and satisfying every wish from birth until about two years of age. Then the child was abandoned by the water well for a long time to develop the value of being self-reliant through the apparent betrayal of others (including family or his tribesmen) who no longer responded to his needs. This story formed my conviction that there is not a time in our lives when we are not surrounded by the worldviews introduced and reinforced to us. The process begins at birth and is presented in the context of family and community. Values and principles that shape the worldview first enter the mind through observations from similar concrete experiences before being distilled into abstract concepts that can more easily connect with observations and conclusions from other areas of experience. Those experiences never leave the brain, nor can they be changed, according to brain research.[2]

Values inevitably become major drivers within worldviews. The immediate effects of Adam's sin resulted in guilt, shame, and fear (Gen 3:7–8) replacing the inherent and sinless values of innocence, honor, and safety. Additionally, Tom Steffen has drawn attention to the value of purity over pollution, which significantly influences the worldviews of Hindus and First Nations people among others. Those from Western cultures often identify more closely to the guilt-innocence categories emphasizing the legal perspective of redemption. Contrastingly, in the majority world there often is greater identification with honor-shame or fear-power categories. Werner Mischke identified a number of cultural dynamics within worldviews that affect human and social relationships and interactions such as patronage, body language, the concept of face, and honor-reversal status that affect the communication of the gospel.[3]

Each of these broad worldview perspectives of value—guilt versus innocence, fear versus power, honor versus shame or pollution versus purity—prompt questions, categorize our observations and responses, and drive people's immediate interpretation of the biblical stories we share. One of the great wonders of the gospel is its response for the guilty, the shamed, the fearful, and the impure revealed through biblical stories. The gospel is broad enough to provide remedy, redemption, and reconciliation for each perspective and need. Sadly, if unfamiliar with the other perspectives, the richness of the gospel's breadth becomes restricted to only a few familiar

---

2. For fuller treatment, see Zull, *Art of Changing the Brain*.
3. For fuller treatment, see Mischke, *Global Gospel*.

perspectives. The breadth of the gospel expands as we become enriched and astonished by the scope and comprehensiveness of the other perspectives we had unintentionally ignored.

Social Construction of Worldviews

Societies collectively organize themselves to protect their community and each member within it according to their beliefs and values—and thus create their own communal cultural worldview. When a problem or threat develops, the members of the society choose a perspective from one of the five foundational institutions of society: government, economics, education, family, and religion. Members of the society propose a solution to any threat according to their preferred perspective. Some define the problem from an economic perspective and propose economic solutions such as capitalism or socialism. Others define the problem from a political perspective and propose democratic or authoritarian governmental solutions. Those who choose the religious perspective look for spiritual remedies. Within each perspective, there will be different solutions available. Consider Elijah confronting the prophets of Baal to determine whose religious worldview—that of Ahab or his own faith in Jehovah—would prove true and provide the prosperity and safety for the nation's future. Both sides saw religion as the critical social institution, but the resolution of which religion to adopt still brought conflict.

Because worldview differences exist among people within the same community, there is a need for gracious conflict resolution. Meeting this need provides another value to using stories. Instead of direct confrontations between two perspectives, impartial stories provide an additional character or situation perspective without personal bias. Instead of a picture of two people arguing directly to each other, you have two people looking together at a story. The resolution—for good or ill—can then be identified and discussed objectively to identify relevant principles from God's perspective that can be personally applied.

The Influence of Words in Constructing Worldview and Stories

Worldview is reflected in the vocabulary chosen to craft our storytelling and our questions and answers. Our vocabulary also reflects our values and beliefs. It's inescapable, but so foundational and unconsciously accepted that it escapes our critical evaluation.

Words reveal what is important to us. When we need a new word, we invent one. Think of all the new tech vocabulary developed in the digital age—words like "Internet," "software," and "mp3"—or discarded words like "cassette" or "8-track." What we don't see as important, we don't communicate. The frequency and number of words we have available to us to describe someone, something, or an experience and its value in our worldview are related. What does this have to do with the Bible?

A missionary colleague invested his life among the First Nations people in the Pacific Northwest. That culture uses around twenty words for snow but has no word for forgiveness. The concept was not in their vocabulary because it wasn't in their community worldview. Interpretive problems arise when another language has several words for something and our own language only has only one word. For example, the Greek language has four words for love—*agape, philia, eros,* and *storgei*—yet English only has one word for all four kinds of love. This may explain why English speakers often confuse their meaning in communicating within relationships.[4]

Because there are values to the words we use to interact with Scripture, we are susceptible to the adage, "What you look for is what you'll get." Jackson Wu provides insight to this inescapable influence of our context upon our interpretation of Scripture. That which Wu identifies as our "cultural lens" is equivalent to what we have been calling "worldview" or "concepts" in this book.

> When reading the Bible, we must recognize that, to some degree, we are all products of our own culture. I am not at all implying some sort of "deterministic" theory of interpretation. Far from it. I simply highlight that cultural contexts inherently influence the kind of things we tend to see and emphasize. We all have a cultural lens. No one reads the Bible completely free of presuppositions that have arisen from (for better or worse) his or her cultural background.[5]

When we explain our perspective to another person in a different culture, we instinctively define the item or the event with the same purpose, priority, and relationships of our own category—but the other person very likely already created different categories for the kind of information offered

---

4. Richards and O'Brien, *Misreading Scripture*, Kindle 1054.
5. Wu, *One Gospel for All Nations*, Kindle 3790.

by us. Because their concerns and needs are different than ours, they may struggle to find where our insights are supposed to be relevant to them and struggle with relating our information to their values, priorities, and relationships. Consequently, we attempt to place possible answers into their categories instead of ours, and the answers might not seem as dramatic as they had just moments earlier. But, unless we make the attempt, our friends may respond with, "Uh, yes. That's very nice." Impact? Negligible!

Consider how systematic theology developed. Questions and observations were collected from the books of the Bible, which were then categorized, grouped together, and interpreted to harmonize with other observations and the categories titled with the suffix -ology (from the Greek *logos*, "word") so it becomes "a word about . . ." theology proper, angelology, soteriology, anthropology, ecclesiology, pneumatology, or eschatology. But these categories reflect the worldview that grouped those observations together. How might other cultures organize and title their own "words about ___" according to their values or perceived relationships? For example, would the study of angels be labeled under a category of "things that can harm you," "what God created," "God's messengers of communication and instruction," or "God's warriors"? How we categorize information will form how we think about that topic according to its purpose, priority and value, and personal relevance to us until those conclusions are challenged and altered as necessary. In other words, the theological category you create or accept becomes part of your personalized definition and that definition is brought into your comprehensive worldview.

Because of this process, the power and relevance of some words of Scripture are overlooked because they did not fit within the familiar worldview of beliefs and values. But when that worldview shifts, then other values need to be considered. The evangelical theologian Timothy Tennent writes:

> Now that Christianity has emerged as a truly global faith and the majority of Christians are located outside the West, we can no longer afford to ignore the discussion of how the traditional understanding of human sin, our guilt before God as sinners, and the redemptive work of Christ on the cross might be best understood and expressed in a shame-based context. This is an important intersection between anthropology and theology that requires further reflection.[6]

---

6. Tennent, *Theology*, Kindle 2577.

PART 2 : COUNTERING NEGATIVE INFLUENCES

The implications of his observation are significant for cross-cultural communication of the gospel! The first implication is that we have to tell stories according to *our listeners'* value perspectives and not *our own*. This isn't a call to develop a new gospel, but rather to enlarge the breadth and relevance of the gospel from our own worldview to communicate its relevance in another. It doesn't change truth, but it expands our understanding of its relevance as it becomes more pointedly revealed within a very different society. The second implication means we will have to use a different vocabulary than that with which we've been comfortable. Tennent draws on an article written by Bruce Nichols to emphasize this issue of overlooking the vocabulary—in this case, the concepts of shame and guilt.

> Bruce Nicholls, the founder of the Evangelical Review of Theology, has acknowledged this problem, noting that Christian theologians have "rarely if ever stressed salvation as honoring God, exposure of sin as shame, and the need for acceptance and the restoration of honor." In fact, a survey of all of the leading textbooks used in teaching systematic theology across the major theological traditions reveals that although the indexes are filled with references to guilt, the word "shame" appears in the index of only one of these textbooks. This omission continues to persist despite the fact that the term guilt and its various derivatives occur 145 times in the Old Testament and 10 times in the New Testament, whereas the term shame and its derivatives occur nearly 300 times in the Old Testament and 45 times in the New Testament.[7]

The third implication is great news: a new vocabulary doesn't need to be developed to tell biblical stories! All the necessary terms have always been in the Bible; the issue has been overlooking words in our storytelling that have had greater meaning and influence in other worldviews—such as shame-based societies—than in a Western-oriented guilt-and-innocence society.

Famed anthropologist, missiologist, author, and professor Miriam Adeney recognized the failure of Western-developed systematic theologies to answer the questions of local cultural issues. New categories of inquiry had to emerge *apart* from the foreign-introduced theological categories to inform the people how to develop new conceptual structures that answered their cultural practices and needs.

7. Tennent, *Theology*, Kindle 2816–23, citing Bruce Nicholls, "The Role of Shame and Guilt in a Theology of Cross-Cultural Missions," *Evangelical Review of Theology* 25/3 (2001) 232.

> Different cultures bring different questions to scripture. "Local theologies" develop these. Take, for example, the titles of the 60 short articles listed in the Africa Bible Commentary's Table of Contents. Would any American commentary contain essays on "Female Genital Mutilation," "Initiation Rites," "The Role of Ancestors," "Widow Inheritance," or "Tribalism, Ethnicity, and Race?" Contexts differ. Therefore, story selections and emphases must differ, based upon wise study of the culture.[8]

Mark Noll identifies the same point with a significant application to sharing the gospel when he writes, "The contrast between the West and the non-West is never between culture-free Christianity and culturally embedded Christianity, but between varieties of culturally embedded Christianity."[9] Distinction between the West and the non-West can be illustrated by the differences in relevance to the listener of a presentation of the gospel emphasizing guilt versus innocence, honor versus shame, pollution versus purity, or fear versus power.

Increasing awareness of how the gospel is relevant to worldviews beyond our personal experiences is really quite an exciting adventure. I previously thought about missions as the *offensive* outreach of the church to those living in darkness. But I now view missions as God's *defense* for the church. By seeing another culture's understanding of the world, the Scriptures, and the impact of Christ within their world, my own blind spots and conceptual presuppositions are exposed and I turn again to ask a question from a different culture's perspective—and often become surprised by scripture's unanticipated answers. For example, when I first learned how communities made collective decisions, I was challenged to know what God said about group and individual decisions—particularly when making a faith decision. I have learned how to linger a bit longer when reading a biblical story that hints at or reveals an honor-shame issue being presented that I would have skipped previously and incorrectly believing the point of the story lay elsewhere. I return to the Scriptures to observe and ask different questions that challenge my ethnocentricity and cultural values of individualism and competition

Often, the instinctive response when answering questions coming from a different worldview is to teach them our familiar words and categories to redefine or replace their familiar words and worldview. We explain the biblical worldview familiar to us because we will always teach as we've

---

8. Adeney in Chiang and Lovejoy, *Beyond Literate Western Models*, Kindle 1336–40.
9. Noll in Mischke, *Global Gospel*, Kindle 891.

been taught, and we expect our listeners to be compelled to agree by the strength of our presentation because, after all, it's what we believe! But it would be a better option to restrain ourselves from teaching from *our* perspective, but encourage our listeners to discover truths that will challenge *their* perspective. That approach might keep us from answering too many questions that nobody is asking.

An example of the connection between words and their categorization is illustrated in the following observation of a cultural value to one of Christianity's most powerful words.

> In Mandarin, the word for "sin" is translated literally as "crime." Therefore, when people hear the gospel, they were being told, "You are criminals!!" Naturally, people do not understand what they are hearing. In China, as in other countries, people think primarily in terms of "face" and relationships. "Law" is less a prominent theme in daily life.
>
> This raised a number of questions.
>
> Theologically, why have Christians favored law-language when so much of the Bible emphasizes God's glory and his people not being put to shame? How could I reconcile the gap between these two metaphors, not choosing one over the other? Why did people get nervous whenever I would talk about honor-shame, as if I were denying what the Bible said about law and absolute truth?[10]

Worldviews become reinforced through a circular reasoning process. The conclusions and conceptual framing of our worldview are supported by the questions we ask that arise from our own worldview. How can a different worldview break the cycle? Is it possible to disrupt this pattern by asking questions from a different perspective that are not interpreted by our reinforced perspective? Or, as Piaget would ask, how do you create a moment of disequilibration that will engage the person to learn something new?

Changing Misconceptions within a Worldview

After several discussions with the late esteemed missiologist Dr. David Hesselgrave about whether education shapes worldview or the worldview shapes teaching, he pointedly challenged me, "Your questioning is like asking which comes first, the chicken or the egg. But the real question you should ask is, 'How do you *change* a worldview as an educator?'"

---

10. Wu, *Saving God's Face*, Kindle 340.

Somehow, the storyteller must disrupt the listeners' assumptions about the story as it is being heard. Remember, the listeners are likely redefining the words to harmonize with their own worldview, dismissing and ignoring contrary concepts as irrelevant, or minimizing the information so it's simply another explanation to explain a point. Without presenting a disruption, or disequilibration, to the thought processes, even biblical stories are vulnerable to misinterpretation.

In the early 1980s, Cornell University supported research about changing misconceptions that produced a curriculum strategy called "conceptual change teaching strategy." To reinforce an earlier statement, a worldview cannot be "changed" by another; it is solely constructed by the holder. The worldview can only be edited, refined, or altered *by the person who created it*. A teacher—or a storyteller—cannot change a person's worldview. Therefore, when speaking of "changing a worldview," we are talking about causing listeners to re-evaluate their present worldview by introducing different contexts and criteria that reveal inadequacies or inconsistencies in their own worldview resulting in influencing them to adapt or reject previous beliefs for a preferred stronger and more consistent or comprehensive worldview.

Conceptual Change Teaching Strategy

One version of a conceptual change teaching strategy proposes four steps taken in a required order to promote a changed worldview. The preparation for the four steps begins with the discipler, teacher, or storyteller recognizing the misconceptions of the listener or the community. Identifying the misconception is essential to define the learning objective for the entire story and lesson design.

The first step requires the learner to become consciously aware of his or her own beliefs about the topic. In Richards and O'Brien's insightful book, *Misreading Scripture with Western Eyes*, the authors frequently refer to the tip-off that someone is gliding over subconscious assumptions when they say or imply ". . . it goes without saying. . ." The assumption—the non-spoken pre-existing worldview—is always the dominant player for interpreting a new story or bit of information, but it is so foundational that it is assumed as a subconscious, unchallenged truth assumption. The assumption must move from the subconscious realm to a conscious level, where it can be identified and challenged.

Part 2 : Countering Negative Influences

I wear eyeglasses. When clean, I find it impossible to look at the glass lens itself while wearing them; I can only look *through* the lens to the world beyond. To actually look *at* the lens, I must remove my glasses and hold them in a way that I can see the glass from a different perspective. That's what has to happen here; the listeners must remove their glasses and look at their worldview lenses from a different perspective. They must bring their values and beliefs to a conscious level.

The second step is the presentation of an alternative perspective that challenges the listener's assumptions. The purpose of this step is to create a sense of the person saying, "I never thought of it like that before."

The third step intentionally presents the new perspective as a plausible and, hopefully, preferable approach or explanation of the event. A characteristic of being plausible is the learner's ability to place himself or herself into this new worldview and recognize how this new perspective solves the deficiencies characteristic of the former worldview. The purpose of authors, movie script writers, and storytellers is to present a character with whom the reader can personally identify and then describe how that character solved or caused a problem. The reader can then safely observe the effects upon the character and evaluate those results from a different perspective.

Finally, the fourth and final step is the learner's recognition of seeing the greater potential and benefit of adopting the new worldview so it is adopted and the previous worldview is consciously rejected. Without consciously rejecting the previous worldview, the newly adopted worldview remains as an available option to use when the setting seems right.

Sometimes, however, the apparent potential and benefit is rejected in favor of competing personal values, such as loyalty to the beliefs of the community or family and the sense of shame that comes with rejecting their ways. Or, like the rich young ruler whom Jesus loved refusing to give up his wealth to follow Jesus (Mark 10:17–23). The decision, in other words, is dependent on other personal influences that override the better choice. The decision always comes from the listener; the storyteller has fulfilled his or her responsibility by presenting and clarifying the contrasts between the choices before the listener (*cf.* Ezek 33:4–6).

These four steps might appear to be too technical or difficult to accomplish. But observe how Jesus modeled this process when he created the story of the Good Samaritan (Luke 10:25–37). Though the teaching moral of the story appears self-evident, there is another level to the passage that exposes Jesus' intention for the story and how he crafted the story lesson, revealing the presence of the four steps toward bringing about change.

The Influence of the Listener's Own Worldview

An expert in the Law asked Jesus what he should do to inherit eternal life. Jesus turned the question back on him, asking how he understood the Law. The expert cited Deuteronomy 6:5, to "love the Lord your God with all your heart and with all your soul and with all your heart." These words are the most precious and well-known to Jews; they follow Deuteronomy 6:4, "*Hear* O Israel; the Lord our God, the Lord is One," which was commanded to be on every Jews' heart, taught to their children, put in a box by their doorpost, and written and bound on their forehead and their arm. This would have been a sufficient and safe response for the expert, but he continued to add a passage from Leviticus 19:18, "you shall love your neighbor as yourself."

Jesus commended this fuller response of the expert and the interchange could have ended there. But the expert wanted to justify himself because he knew he did not personally measure up to the standard of love expected. As a legal expert, he knew a loophole, and wondered aloud, "And who is my neighbor?" Jesus was familiar with the loophole and heard his justification. So Jesus chose to create a lesson to challenge the spiritually fatal misconception that redefined the intended meaning of the Law.

The legal loophole was based on the definition of "neighbor" because two different Hebrew words were used for "neighbor" within the five-verse passage in Leviticus that the teacher cited. In Leviticus 19:13–18, five commands are given to govern relationships with neighbors: you shall not oppress your neighbor . . . you are to judge your neighbor fairly . . . you are not to act against the life of your neighbor . . . you may surely reprove your neighbor, but shall not incur sin because of him [and] . . . you shall love your neighbor as yourself (v. 18). The more common word for "neighbor" was *rea*—a word that communicated a friend or companion, someone with whom there was a personal, friendly relationship. The other word, *amith*, communicated an associate, a fellow with whom there was a relationship but more nuanced toward having equivalent status than a personal relationship. *Amith* was used in Leviticus 19:15 concerning judging a neighbor fairly, and in 19:17 to justify correcting a neighbor but without hatred. Obviously there is a very subtle but critical difference between these two words. The single Greek word used in Luke's passage and elsewhere in the Septuagint carried the extended application of a heart relationship represented by *rea*.

Early in the Jewish history, this expectation of "loving your neighbor as much as yourself" became restricted to only those within the

Part 2 : Countering Negative Influences

covenant—that is, a neighbor who held equal status within the covenant. If the person wasn't part of the covenant, the Jew was not required to love the other as himself according to the teachers of the Law. During Jesus' time, the Qumran community further limited the application of neighborly love only to other Qumran members and not even to other Jews who weren't members of Qumran. Contrastingly, Jesus expected the application of love to extend beyond such restrictions to include loving all others as self as a personal quality to inherit eternal life.

The New Testament scholar I. Howard Marshall, when commenting about this understanding of *rea*, wrote:

> The Jews interpreted this in terms of members of the same people and religious community fellow-Jews (cf. Mt. 5:43–48). There was a tendency on the part of the Pharisees to exclude the ordinary people from the definition, and the Qumran community excluded those whom they termed 'the sons of darkness' . . . but Jewish usage excluded Samaritans and foreigners from this category.[11]

Jesus would not allow the teacher to use the loophole to justify himself! So he created a story and gave us a pattern to follow: 1) listen closely to the person's responses, 2) identify any misconception(s), 3) select or construct a story to challenge the misconception, 4) tell the story, and 5) call for a personal evaluation and commitment.

Jesus' story lesson also reflected the conceptual change teaching strategy: 1) prompt the listener to elevate his own beliefs, values, or worldview at a conscious level, 2) present an alternative perspective, 3) demonstrate the preference of the new perspective over the former perspective, and 4) reject the former conceptual understanding and accept the new understanding.

Jesus prompted the teacher to elevate his beliefs to a conscious level by describing the responses of the priest and the Levite to the stricken victim (Luke 10:31–32). The teacher probably identified with the actions of the priest and Levite and would have done the same thing to avoid the potential of becoming unclean without any responsibility or love to this victim who did not qualify as a neighbor. In doing so, the expert raised his values and beliefs to a conscious level.

The second step of the process calls for presenting a contrasting perspective. Jesus dramatically changed the scenario by introducing a compassionate response to help by—of all people—a Samaritan. Why a Samaritan? This represented a person who was totally disqualified from either of the

11. Marshall, *Commentary on Luke*, 444.

The Influence of the Listener's Own Worldview

criteria used by the expert. He had no personal relationship (*rea*) or equal status (*amith*) with the Jews. There was a different criteria for neighbor; the expert had even named it himself earlier for which he was commended. But, he defined the word "love" in his worldview to be deprived of the despised. Jesus approached the issue through a question to recognize the inclusivity of the despised and to apply the principle neither to the status or relationship of the other person, but to the compassionate character of the neighborly person.

So, the third step—recognizing the contrasting responses coming from two competing worldviews—was begun by Jesus asking the expert, "Which of these three [Levite, priest, or Samaritan] proved to be a neighbor to the man who fell into the robbers hands?" (Luke 10:36). Notice that Jesus did not ask the expert what he would have done—which could have led to a second defensive or self-justifying answer—but rather deflected the question to a neutral evaluation of the responses of the three characters. It's not enough to tell the story; the challenge of worldview change is dependent upon a personal challenge, discussion, and decision as a part of the oral story lesson. In this case, for the expert to answer Jesus' question with either the priest or the Levite's response would have been absurd, which worked deeply into his conceptual framework and challenged him to change his worldview and, ultimately, his response.

The fourth step—rejecting the former worldview and accepting the new worldview—was affirmed when Jesus heard the expert's answer that the neighbor was the one who acts compassionately, to which Jesus replied with the command, "Go and do the same." That command caused the rejection of the teacher's former perspective.

If we focus only on the content of Jesus' teaching in passages such as this, we can overlook *why* Jesus taught a particular story or responded as he did. Rather, by identifying and emphasizing the specific misconception that prompted his teaching or response, we are able to recognize the misconception as it appears in our own contemporary situations and—*based upon the similarities of the misconception found in the scripture and in the person before us*—be able to respond to the person's need or weakness as Jesus would. Failure to appreciate this personal *connection through misconception* reveals the wrong conclusion that those listening to us only need to know the facts of the story instead of also understanding *why* the answer fits the need. Taking the time to clearly describe the misconception is the surest help to guide the how and why of our own response.

PART 2 : COUNTERING NEGATIVE INFLUENCES

Reflecting on questions that bring focus to the person's personal misconception increases our ability to teach or tell the story with greater impact because of our sensitivity to prompt our listeners to identify their own beliefs as they identify with the disciples and discover solutions and alternative explanations through their stories.

Use Caution When Identifying Others' Perspectives as Misconceptions

To identify and label misconceptions in another's worldview requires great humility and the passion of a learner. Every teacher has learned from another—which means teachers *also* draw their understanding from *their* prior learning and values. So, before we teachers critique another's worldview for their cultural influences, we must also become aware of our own cultural influences—and we are just as blind to our own influences as we accuse others of being blind to theirs. How do we escape our own blindspots? Through Christian missions. The more we are exposed to other cultures' expressions of Christianity, the more we are forced to recognize our own cultural glasses as our interactions encourage questioning our own assumptions to see if they are truly biblical or our own cultural accretions.

The universal church has a responsibility to hold each other accountable to Romans 12:2: "And do not be conformed to this world, but be transformed by the renewing of your mind, so that you may prove what the will of God is, that which is good and acceptable and perfect." Seeing how Christians in other cultures work out their own salvation and their spiritual practices in obedience oftentimes leads us into the process of self-evaluating our own practices—perhaps instilling a bit more flexibility to our interpretations or causing us to recognize applications we never saw before. These all help our spiritual integrity and make more glorious the revelation of God's words to us.

The key point is to teach humbly in a way that recognizes the presence of errors in an existing worldview and address them in a manner that encourages the learner to both *recognize* and *resolve* competing ideas so that it weakens or destroys the influence of error and prevents the development of syncretism—the mixing of truth and error. New information does not easily replace old information. Old information is persistent information; it's a survivor!

Without intentionally applying teaching strategies that are able to cause acceptance of a biblical worldview, the new information—or the story—will either 1) be redefined to accommodate the conceptual structure of the learner's existing worldview, 2) serve as an alternative explanation in a different situation, or 3) be ignored as being irrelevant because there was no place where it appeared applicable. The first two reactions will often lead to syncretism and the third response leads to nothing at all. Those are discouraging options! We cannot ignore existing faulty worldviews by simply assuming they will cease as truth is embraced. Their persistence requires our intentional efforts to cause the learner to recognize the errors and consciously reject error and be committed to truth.

Chapter Summary

The objective of this book is to encourage spiritual generations to multiply by enabling each generation to teach others also. However, negative influences can hinder reproductive multiplication. Two of the negative influences affecting our educational strategy and their remedies have been presented: first, use oral learning methods instead of literate methods to reach oral-preference learners; second, use conceptual change teaching strategies to challenge the persistence of pre-existing worldviews of the listeners.

Everyone wants to be successful and thrive; it's a natural instinct! But to be successful and thrive we must decide if the world around us is a friendly, supportive environment or a hostile, antagonistic environment that must be manipulated or defeated. To make that decision requires observation of the actions of the world on our path and make decisions accordingly. That's so much information that our brain uses a strategy of sorting and categorizing information into similar categories or topics. These categories relate to other categories to construct larger concepts that explain and answer our questions about heritage, behaviors, values, and beliefs into a more comprehensive conceptual structure (worldview) that provides a safe way for us to interact with our world.

Because worldviews are individually constructed and influenced by family, community, and schooling, misconceptions will inevitably form. But when new information challenges these misconceptions, one of three responses is common: the new information is manipulated to fit into existing concepts, evaluated and ignored as irrelevant, or remembered as a nice moral story despite having no eternal influence. A different strategy—conceptual change teaching strategy—is a four-step educational process that compels the learner to recognize and reject error and embrace a biblical worldview as a better solution to personal and social problems.

Chapter 5

The Influence of the Storyteller Assuming the Role of Teacher

THE PHARISEES AND THE scribes complained that Jesus' disciples were not following the traditions of the elders—specifically, that they did not ceremonially wash their hands when eating. Jesus responded by accusing them of violating the commands of God because of their traditions. He gave an example of such an error when they dedicate money to the temple treasury rather than upholding God's command to honor their father and mother by providing money to help them instead. Jesus called them hypocrites and referred to Isaiah's charge, "This people honors Me with their lips, but their heart is far away from Me. Their worship is useless to me as they teach as doctrines the instructions of men" (Matt 15:1–9).

How could these leaders become guilty of such a charge by Jesus? The Pharisees were well known and self-righteously proud of their detailed upholding of the Law, so how could it happen that their teachings would violate the Law they said they loved above all else?

The Pharisees believed in the Law's authority, but they taught what the Law *meant* and assumed the role as the exclusive interpreters of the Law's meaning for themselves. In doing so, they transferred the Law's authority from the Scriptures to themselves as they "(taught) as doctrines the instructions of men." An attribute proving God as the source of Scripture is that Scripture never contradicts itself. However, when men begin to add authoritative interpretations and develop traditions to reinforce their personal beliefs, the interpretations eventually reveal their human source by adopting inevitable contradictions. And Jesus exposed how their human

The Storyteller Assuming the Role of Teacher

interpretations and traditions eventually added to and then contradicted the Law.

This potential can happen in oral biblical storying. Storytellers and story crafters must distinguish between what the scripture says from the personal opinions added to help make the scripture understandable. Stories should always be verified and compared with Scripture. It is when various personal beliefs and meanings are added to the story—no matter how well intentioned the purpose is—that the practice of repeating these additions will ultimately lead to confusion of what the Bible truly says. It is always and only the biblical story that is authoritative.

If storytellers add interpretations, confusion of what the scripture actually says will multiply in the process of retelling through the generations. This happened centuries ago in the early church when monks, serving as copyists, would add words to aid explanation of a difficult text. Then those texts with additions would be copied as if they were the original text. This scholarly practice to identify the original biblical text from added material is called textual criticism. A usual consideration to choose the original text is to favor the more difficult reading because it is unlikely that monks would add words to make the text more confusing. Each spiritual generation must protect what is Scripture apart from explaining meanings of the text. Other books or commentaries propose interpretive meanings but explanations should not become confused with the biblical text. Not only is this distinction good theology, it directly impacts the strategy of generational spiritual multiplication.

Adding personal perspectives, though well intentioned, shifts authority from the Scriptures to the Pharisee, interpreter, or teacher. It also supplants the role of the Holy Spirit to illuminate Scripture to the believer. The storyteller tends to explain the meaning from the perspective of what makes sense in his or her own context rather than what the Holy Spirit intends from the listener's context.

The role of the storyteller is to be a facilitator to discuss the story and not become the authoritative source of the story—which was the trap that caught the Pharisees. What stops a storyteller from taking the dangerous shortcut of adding personal opinions or additional biblical material outside the story to teach the meaning of the story in addition to the story itself? There *is* a remedy and it begins with being clear about the differences between the role of the teacher and the role of the storyteller.

PART 2 : COUNTERING NEGATIVE INFLUENCES

The Hebrew Understanding of Teaching

The most common Old Testament Hebrew word group translated "to teach" is *yada*. *Yada* means "to know," but when the verb appears in its causative form, it makes the word literally mean "cause to know," which is usually translated as "teach." This means that God's chosen word for "teach" is not merely to pass along information, but "to cause the person to know." The application should be that we haven't taught or passed on truth until we have caused the other person to know. That changes the question from "What content do I teach?" or "How do I get the listener to repeat what I believe?" to "How do I cause the person to know?"

How does that meaning of "teach" harmonize with Piaget's processes of *disequilibration, accommodation, assimilation,* and *equilibration* introduced in chapter 4? The process begins when a misconception held by a character within the story is exposed and the same misconception appears to be held by the listener. The "causing to know" teaching experience begins by telling the story to the listener. As the biblical character faces increasing judgment or experiences the effects of the misconceptions, the listener—through involvement with the story—will hopefully identify with the character and recognize the experiences in his or her own life and see how the events play out in the story.

The listener may experience some discomfort in identifying with the biblical character or event. Theologically, we identify this discomfort as coming under the conviction of the Holy Spirit through hearing the Word of God. Educationally, we say the listener is feeling a disequilibration that seeks resolution. The disequilibration can be resolved by making a decision to assimilate the new perspective or information and adjust the personal worldview and choose to live in obedience to Scripture. Or the listener can evaluate whether change would help their situation and choose to live with knowing both options while postponing the decision. The storyteller doesn't need to argue or defend a way of resolution; simply continue to discuss the story in a non-aggressive manner and encourage discussion through good questions. This responsibility of the storyteller can be fulfilled by a new believer or even a non-believer. The power to change or repent comes from the story and the Holy Spirit and not even from the spiritual maturity of the storyteller. That's exciting!

The Storyteller Assuming the Role of Teacher

The Role of the Storyteller

Jesus was often addressed as "teacher" (*didaskale*) and *rabbi*—a term referring to "master" but also later applied as a sign of respect for scribes and teachers of God's Law. But Jesus clearly commanded, "Do not be called rabbi; for One is your Teacher, and you are all brothers" (Matt 23:8). The context of these prohibitions is to warn against seeking such highly respected and grand titles or assuming a superior role to others. We should, instead, acknowledge our relationships as brothers to one another, for we have one heavenly Father and our leader is Christ. Our attitude should be to serve one another (Matt 23:11–12)!

Jesus frequently selected stories as a non-aggressive method to challenge the beliefs of people holding misconceptions. His storytelling did not reveal an attitude of being authoritative as master or leader, but modeled how to come alongside and use a story to expose errors in thinking.

Discussions encouraged by questions about the story—rather than challenging the listeners directly—can uncover patterns of sloppy thinking to be clarified, inconsistent answers to be reconciled, occasional lapses of logic previously ignored but now apparent, or an unhealthy reliance upon statements that are little more than slogans that, after exposure, must all be resolved. The role of the storyteller is to faithfully tell the story (without addition or explanation) and facilitate discussion leading to self-discovery of an inconsistency that unbalances—or disequilibrates—the listeners' existing worldview.

Jesus obviously had much information about himself and the Father he could have shared. But he restrained himself from providing what would have been astonishing information. Instead, he was more interested in asking questions to open the way toward discussion that could lead to the listener's self-discovery of truth. Once again, visualize the concept of dialogue by comparing two scenes. The first scene places two chairs facing each other, with the storyteller in one chair and the listener in the other and the story being between them. In the second scene, the chairs are side by side and the story is in front of both the storyteller and listener. The purpose of these two visualizations is to eliminate any sense of an adversarial role. The goal is to be two people equally analyzing the biblical story together. That's the best approach to envision and the approach to take whether it's talking with one person or a group.

The storyteller cannot be effective in causing listeners to discover the truths they needed if he or she assumes a dominant role. The process must be learner centered because it is the learner alone who makes the personal worldview decisions. A dominating teacher is simply trying to out prove, out think, out argue, or out promote his or her own worldview. A storytelling teacher allows the listener to grapple with the story to discover where the inconsistencies with personal beliefs might differ. But how does a storyteller present such a learner-centered discussion?

Creating the Environment for Adult Learning

The following ten principles and practices are essential to creating an environment that encourages learning engagement among adults. These principles were either identified or inspired by the esteemed adult educator Dr. Jane Vella, and applied here specifically to learner-centered discussion to encourage reproduction.[1] Modeling these principles while telling and discussing a story enables the listener to recognize how to avoid being an "expert." When all that is expected of a new believer is to tell a story just heard and to encourage discussion, the lack of expecting an authoritative or knowledgeable role increases the likelihood the person will tell the story to other friends—which is critical strategic generational multiplication.

1. Positive relationships between the teacher and learner and among all the learners. Understanding learning as a social event means there must be a positive relationship between the teacher and the learner.

2. Safety in the environment and the process. Safety is not referring here to the physical safety of the learners—though in some of your situations that could be an issue. Instead, this refers to both the mental and emotional issues of safety that encourages open discussion—particularly when people feel it is safe to speak their feelings and beliefs before a group of people.

3. Therefore, if the storyteller is before a group of listeners, there must be guidance about how people can disagree without being disagreeable. This requires modeling how to respond to each other with phrases like, "I'm not sure I understood you, correctly. Could you rephrase that?" Or, "I liked your point on this, but I'm not sure I understand this other point enough to agree or disagree with you about it yet." Or, "I'm not sure I agree with your position yet; I need to think about it. This

---

[1]. See Vella, *Learning to Listen, Learning to Teach*.

The Storyteller Assuming the Role of Teacher

is how I would characterize it. What's your reaction to my thoughts?" Remember that dialogical teaching needs to be interactive—within a safe environment—which leads to evaluation and critical thinking and results in choosing the best ideas without fear of loss of personal status or possible rejection from the group.

4. Using questions is an extremely powerful and effective strategy that was presented more fully in chapter 1. The construction of questions is culturally influenced and directly affects the information processing of oral learners. The use of questions not only requires skillful crafting but also sharpened sensitivity to the leading of the Holy Spirit on whether to initiate questions or wait for his leading and possible delay.

5. Engagement of the learners in what they are learning. The primary task of a facilitator is to keep everyone in the group interacting with each other. In some cultures, it is respectful not to speak for oneself and allow only the eldest of the group to respond for the group. In other cultures, asking a question of the storyteller—though specifically requested to ask a question—would be an insult for it would indicate the storyteller did not tell the story well enough for the listener to still have a question. In some cultures, it is a sign of great disrespect to ask questions of a holy book. Obviously, then, engaging conversations must reflect cultural standards and may require only person-to-person discussions at either an earlier or later time than with the group.

6. Remember that *every* person has the potential of reaching hundreds of people through their spiritual generation line, so a goal of the facilitator is not to lose anyone from the discussion; everyone must be kept engaged. If discussion is uncomfortable for some, have everyone in the group draw a picture about what comes to mind visually when the topic is discussed. Be creative! If it's through singing, then make the song! If it's through dancing, then make the dance! Everyone must be engaged in what they are learning.

7. Respect for learners as decision-makers. Adults need to be respected as decision-makers—having the power to determine what they want to learn for themselves o, even choose what to discuss in these learning discussions. For example, new information can be brought into the discussion by asking, "What else do you feel you need to learn about this topic?" This allows the content to be an open system that invites

Part 2 : Countering Negative Influences

critical analysis and, most importantly, how they see the information connect with their need. Allowing the learners to be decision-makers of what they're learning not only permits making new information relevant to their need but also provides the freedom and motivation to continue to explore the information. Don't confuse these decisions with rejecting the curriculum; they are adjusting the curriculum enough to create an ownership of what they are learning and adopting for themselves.

8. Practice action with reflection or learning by doing. There are three aspects to learning: ideas, feelings, and actions. Concentrating only on the ideas and information can become irrelevant to the actions of our lives. If trying to lead someone or the group toward a response as an application to a concept, be sure to ask about the learner's feelings about it before doing some activity or application. The more you can encourage the learners to become comfortable with the idea, their feelings, and their active response, the more easily the idea becomes owned and brought into their lives. This will keep the lessons from becoming fragmented and irrelevant and keep the relationship between knowing, being and doing strongly connected. This approach focuses adults to practice action with reflection, or learning by doing.

9. Teach for learning that is immediately applicable. Do not begin to talk about abstract ideas or teach things that would likely only surface three or four years down the road. Always ask what the learners need to know *now* for *this* time in their lives. If it is difficult to express how your learner should apply what is being learned the next week, then drop the topic and choose something else to discuss.

10. Require accountability. Accountability answers the question, "How do they know they know?" The answer is . . . if they can teach it! Depending on how well the story is taught—incorporating ideas, feelings, and actions—the learner will grow in confidence that he or she really knows, understands, applies, and can create new ways of learning.

A powerful influence that discourages new believers from immediately sharing and discussing biblical stories with their personal network of friends is the fear of the expectation to know more than they actually do. It is an unbelievable weight to bear if new believers are either expected to know or assume the personal responsibility of being a source for explaining Christianity. That's an intimidating role to play! However, if the new

The Storyteller Assuming the Role of Teacher

believer is not expected to assume that role, but only requested to share a story and discuss it with a friend in a non-judgmental environment as presented here, the intimidation would decrease if not become eliminated—increasing the likelihood of retelling the story. Requested answers can always be delayed by the response, "That's interesting. I don't know, but I'll see what others say and get back to you."

Chapter Summary

The objective of this book is to encourage spiritual generations to multiply by enabling each generation to teach others through storytelling. Three negative influences that could hinder the new convert's motivation or willingness to retell biblical stories could be counteracted by three educational design decisions: 1) use oral learning methods to reach other oral-preference learners; 2) use conceptual change teaching strategies to challenge the persistence of pre-existing worldviews of the listeners; and 3) use learner-centered storytelling and facilitate discussion about the stories.

Storytellers must resist the temptation to tell listeners what the meaning of the story is. That's not the role of the storyteller! Adding any information to the story confuses what the sacred story is with what is opinion, despite having sincere intentions. To add information makes the storyteller the authority instead of the story itself. The multiplication strategy for retelling the story to others also multiplies the "story-plus-opinion" version for future spiritual generations, which multiplies the variety of versions and makes review of a story against the biblical source difficult.

Jesus spoke against the scribes and rabbis, who assumed the authoritative role in interpreting meaning according to their own doctrines of man. Jesus' view was that we should be of equal relationship under God our Father and as brothers and sisters of each other. Therefore, the storyteller should assume the role of a facilitator, empowered by the Holy Spirit, to discuss the story and ask questions to encourage the listeners to discover the meaning and application of the story together. The storyteller can cause the listener to learn by creating a learner-centered environment that allows for a variety of objectives to encourage listeners to discuss with one another.

Chapter 6

The Influence of Addition Instead of Multiplication Processes

THE PREVIOUS THREE CURRICULUM design proposals affected educational strategies. These next two chapters describe influences negatively affecting the reproduction of storytellers and story crafters. The goal is to multiply storytellers and story crafters through coming generations. It is possible, however, to unintentionally adopt addition processes.

The earliest beginning of the church appears to depend on addition processes:

- Acts 2:41: " . . . and that day there were added about 3,000 souls"
- Acts 2:47: " . . . and the Lord was adding to their number day by day . . ."
- Acts 4:4: "But many of those who heard the message (from Peter and John) believed; and the number of the men came to be about five thousand."
- Acts 5:14: "multitudes of men and women were constantly added to their number"

Addition processes accelerate rapid initial growth, but the growth rate is usually not sustainable. Growth by addition usually reflects initial dependence upon a single, visionary leader. The single leader is the most effective spokesperson to champion a new vision and possess the necessary leadership charisma to recruit a team, group, or followers to that vision. In the infant church's case, these initial growth spurts appear directly related to the leadership of the Apostle Peter. Though a single leader offers great reward, dependence upon one person also brings great risk. For example, without peer accountability the single leader is vulnerable to character and spiritual temptations or flaws—such as pride, power, arrogance, or disobedience—that can disqualify the person from continuing to lead. Obviously, this particular vulnerability was not an inevitable consequence, as evidenced by Peter and other successful pastoral leaders who placed themselves under mutual accountability with others.

But the single leader is also vulnerable to events and conditions beyond his or her control or influence that can result in premature removal—events like illness or death, financial stress, government, or persecution. The single leader becomes a target of the enemy, which happened to Peter when King Herod imprisoned him to be executed when Passover ended (Acts 12:11–17). Following the miraculous angelic intervention that released Peter from prison but also prompted his immediate departure from Jerusalem, the biblical narrative shifts to the missionary team of Barnabas and Paul, sent out by the church of Antioch. The Jerusalem church's next reference to leadership comes through the direction of the team of apostles and leaders (Acts 15:23) under James as the new leader.

But Jesus referred to a different mathematical process than addition when he taught about growth in the parable of the soils (Matt 13:1–9). The climax of the story came when he spoke of the seed that " . . . fell on the good soil and yielded a crop, some a hundredfold, some sixty, and some thirty" (Matt 13:8).

The root word *rabah*, translated as "multiply," appears over two hundred times in the Old Testament, being adopted from other, older languages, where it means "much," "many," or "great." In other verses, the word is translated as "gather much," "give more," "yield much," and "heap." *Rabah* is therefore not referring to a specific mathematic process, but to communicate God's promise to increase quickly the generations of Abraham's descendants. God always intends the yield of his harvests to be great, abundant, and overflowing. It is, nonetheless, worthwhile to compare the processes of addition and multiplication to identify processes of growth that are different; their differences reveal differences in harvest yields.

What could change the somewhat predictable results from adding second-generation converts to the "great yield" that results in exponential multiplication through the third, fourth, and unlimited generations? What trait is critical to monitor to change the process of one evangelist reaching

PART 2 : COUNTERING NEGATIVE INFLUENCES

one convert in a "one generation and done" cycle of addition instead of multiplying and continuing "multiple generations and continuing" cycles to thirty- or hundredfold increases?

Discerning Addition or Multiplication Processes

Using the addition process of 3+3+3=9 produces the same outcome as the multiplication process of 3x3=9. Numeric comparisons of results done too early can mislead and assume that multiplication rather than addition processes are being used. For example, Bob taught a Bible study to seven people overseas. Bob then taught another group of nine and then a third group of eight participants. When he returned home from his teaching trip, Bob reported to his supporters, "I've multiplied my ministry twenty-four times." Would that be true?

The correct answer is "probably not." *Multiplication is not telling other people what you know, but enabling other people to do what you did.* If all twenty-four of those people taught others as Bob taught them, then he would have indeed multiplied himself twenty-four times. But that was unlikely. Perhaps they applied what Bob taught them personally. That would be encouraging to Bob—but he hadn't replaced himself. Bob might have added others who now know what he knew, but that wouldn't be multiplication. Not until they are enabled to do what he did—without him being there—would there be multiplication. Leading a person to faith in Jesus Christ is an addition strategy; it does not become multiplication until that person is equipped and successful to lead another person to faith in the same way.

Replacement is, therefore, the key observable trait that distinguishes between addition and multiplication. If the first-generation evangelist taught a second-generation convert, who or what must be replaced to ensure multiplication and not addition is happening? If the faithful new convert has the ability to teach another, the first-generation evangelist is being replaced. The first-generation evangelist is free to begin another generational line as the convert also begins a new lineage. What produces the rapid and great harvest is the rapid number of evangelists who replace themselves by enabling others to do what they did. The answer appears to be logical, so why doesn't it happen more naturally? Why does the default process appear to be addition for new ministry initiatives?

Influence of Addition Instead of Multiplication

A burdened, vision-filled evangelist often begins a ministry initiative using techniques or processes that naturally fit his or her own skills, abilities, and temperament. The missionary is encouraged by the fruit of new converts and models the process and technique for the new converts, who affirm the evangelist's vision and learn his skills. However, the convert's skill, ability, and temperament may not match those of the evangelist and discouragement from a lack of fruitful responses may lead them to conclude they are not gifted and unable to reproduce a new potential generation.

Because of the evangelist's personal ministry success in producing second-generation converts and disciples, there is a mistaken assumption that the evangelist is multiplying his ministry despite the absence of third-generation believers. But if the evangelist has not replaced himself and the hope of new converts or new disciples remains dependent upon him, the ministry is using growth by addition. Addition is an *event*—or a series of events—that promise immediate results. Contrastingly, multiplication is a *process* based upon replacement with results initially appearing more slowly.

One teacher will always be inadequate no matter how many learners are taught; there is always a need to keep producing and replacing new disciple-makers. The first-generation evangelist must do more than pass on the ministry skills of his message, but must also pass on his or her responsibility and ownership. The Brazilian educator Paulo Freire declared, "Only the student can name the moment of the death of the professor." This is the moment when the disciple is confident in his or her own competence and can even question, disagree, or challenge the discipler. Such discussions are an indication of the learner taking ownership of the initiative and should not be feared—if the discussion doesn't lead to unproductive splits. It is evidence of the beginning of great learning by the new student.

Advocating personal replacement is not advocating replacement of existing pastoral authority. Where the organized church is already present, replacement refers to replacing many of the pastors' functional activities, including teaching and disciple-making. But the pastor remains the responsible authority as shepherd of the people and should not be threatened by developing other leadership within the church—leaders who are capable and empowered to assist the pastor with his evangelistic ministry. Pastoral authority should grow at a slower pace, using internship, experience, and proof of servant mentality with validation of his calling to the role.

The apostles recognized the distinction between leadership and teaching authority and responsibility as they established the role of deacons.

Jesus is the only head of the church; it is too big a responsibility for any one person. The local pastor-teacher needs the help of others who come alongside, but those others need to be developed by the pastor and the pastor never loses the responsibility to oversee their efforts.

One of the great temptations faced by competent leaders or teachers is prompted by the question, "Well, who will do this if I don't? There aren't enough other disciplers or evangelists available for such a vision!" Where does the fault of inadequate numbers of leaders or teachers lie? How did Jesus address that question?

Jesus acknowledged that "it is to your advantage that I go away" (John 16:7). It wouldn't have been an advantage to them if Jesus left too early. But it was an advantage as soon as he concluded his disciples had learned all they needed to know to provide the leadership and vision the church would need. He knew they were ready because he personally discipled them.

To decide it was an advantage for him to leave meant it had become a liability for him to remain—an awesome thought! He needed to leave for a variety of reasons—among which is recognizing that more can be done if the evangelist is replaced because the convert is enabled and entrusted to do what the evangelist modeled and taught.

This is not an easy decision for a leader to make! The leader had invested lengthy and sometimes painful effort to disciple the new disciple, only to make a decision to leave just prior to the fruitful harvest! Who wouldn't want to finally be a part of the joyful harvest and see the reward of all that labor? But instead, the evangelist's expected hope and celebration of the reward is not to be crowds of new believers, but crowds of new discipler-makers and storytellers of the third and following spiritual generations enlarging the kingdom.

But the leader might be tempted to retain authority and control for his own glory. Pastor David currently serves in his home European country, where he pastors the only evangelical church in a 300-kilometer radius. Though there were only 150 people in his congregation, he prays regularly to see his church grow to 10,000. When asked the question, "Would it be better to have one church of 10,000 under one pastor or have 1,000 churches of ten each, with 1,000 pastors?" he was unable—or unwilling—to reply. He was pressed with another question: "If you pastored 10,000 people, would you find your time being devoted to administration and pastoral care so that you neglected the continuing need for apostolic outreach? What if, instead, you could disciple five men who learned how to disciple others and learned how to care for others? Which church could better escape persecution? Which church would be better able to survive if something happened to your health? Which church would not require outside financial support?" Pastor David still hasn't expressed a commitment toward this different expression of the church. This perspective is not a statement that there is no place for a large church; that is an issue of God's determination. But churches that are large for the leaders' own glory and do not seek to multiply other leaders to replace themselves might want to periodically evaluate their own motives.

Jesus did not wait until he saw thousands of believers in his kingdom; he had "accomplished the work which You (the Father) have given me to do" (John 17:4). So he postponed the joy of experiencing the harvest from every tribe, tongue and nation—and instead reported to the Father, "As You sent Me into the world, I also have sent them into the world" (John 17:18). The Apostle John understood the impact of Jesus' words when, about sixty years later, he wrote, "I have no greater joy than this, to hear of my children walking in the truth" (3 John 4). There is nothing more exciting for an evangelist than to see spiritual children reproducing spiritual grandchildren. But there is great temptation to remain intimately involved in the harvest. But the model of Jesus is clear: Identify the faithful and enable them to teach others. When they are able, it's time to leave them as empowered evangelists and teachers to handle the harvest to come—not to remain and disadvantage them. The models of Jesus and Paul should shape our prayers to be, "Give me ten faithful men *who are able to reproduce* what they had learned to a third generation rather than hundreds, or even thousands, who affirm their beliefs but *who are unable to reproduce.*"

Educational Design and Multiplication

A multiplication strategy that depends on new believers to share their faith immediately with their friends requires a supporting curriculum capable of overcoming their fears, inhibitions, and obvious knowledge limitations. Lacking confidence in their knowledge and their ability to present their faith, a new believer is unlikely to share the gospel. The curriculum design must fill that vacancy. What new believers *can* know and communicate with confidence is a biblical story and how to discuss the story with their friends using questions as they assume the role of a facilitator instead of a mature believer. The story and the storyteller are the curriculum. And this curriculum can be easily and consistently modeled to succeeding spiritual generations.

The minimum curriculum design requirements for story lessons are that they be short, simple, easily reproduced, and memorable. Remain focused on the goal of the lesson—which is not to train future leaders of the church but to rapidly introduce their friends to the stories of God's actions. There is a temptation for curriculum developers to produce lessons suitable for training the next generation of "Pauls"—the next leaders. Instead, the lessons should be designed to reach the third generation, "faithful men" who are able to tell stories to others.

Assuredly, there will come a time to train "Pauls," but training leaders takes time whereas reproducing stories about Jesus must begin immediately and spread as rapidly as any rumor within the community. A quick, fast-paced curriculum will be unsuccessful when aimed toward leadership development. Jesus took three years to develop his leaders, and he was the master teacher. Future leaders cannot leapfrog over evangelism but must go through the rapidly reproducing evangelism program of storytelling to experience the process themselves and develop their passion for the lost before assuming leadership responsibilities. The continuing training for leaders must be secondary or the primary benefits of the rapid growth are lost, which is addressed more completely in chapter 9.

The Impact of Dependent Resources Limiting Multiplication

Selecting a multiplying ministry strategy dependent upon printed materials such as books, tracts, and pamphlets requires multiplying financial resources and reduces the role of a new believer to be a dependent deliverer rather than a dynamic witness. *Multiplication cannot progress faster than the multiplying rate of producing any required resources.* Could it be that the church multiplied itself faster in the first century because it was not forced to multiply additional resources?

By contrast, the ability to reproduce biblical stories exponentially for generations without dependence on printed resources eliminates exponentially increasing financial challenges. Eliminating the time and financial expenses for translation expenses and printing and delivering materials—often in hostile contexts—is a distinct advantage for oral storying.

Acknowledging the faster and broader possibilities of reaching more people with God's stories through multiplication is only half of the reproductive strategy. Multiplication can be slowed or stopped by limiting storytelling to only mature believers. Storytelling is not a process to be delayed by restricting the telling to only mature believers. Rather, storytelling needs to be encouraged among new believers, the subject of the next chapter.

Chapter Summary

Ministry initiatives often begin through the efforts of a single visionary leader with the ability to recruit others to join in the vision. But a ministry's future sustainability is jeopardized if it continues to depend on the single leader. The leader is susceptible to personal failings that can result in removal from the ministry or because the leader becomes a vulnerable target of the enemy resulting in governmental persecution, visa problems or financial stresses. The Apostle Peter had to leave the Jerusalem ministry due to becoming an enemy of Herod—leading toward his execution except for the miraculous intervention of an angel.

Rapid, multiplying ministry growth enables developing other leaders who can assume the responsibility for the ministry in the event a leader is removed. The primary indication of the active presence of multiplication is the leader's ability and willingness to replace himself with others. The leader's willingness to replace himself is tested by overcoming the temptations of prematurely enjoying the potentially fruitful harvest, the personal reward of fame and glory associated with leading a fruitful ministry, or the lack of trusting a new disciple to minister as a peer colleague. Jesus knew it would be better for his disciples that he depart from them than remain for the joy of the harvest. Jesus knew that his work was complete in seeing a few disciples prepared for leadership roles rather than the criteria of thousands of believers without enough prepared leaders.

A multiplying strategy requires an educational strategy that won't limit its pattern of growth. If the harvest exhibited exponential growth, then the supporting educational resources must also grow exponentially. The most effective solution is to reduce or eliminate resource dependence. And that is the great advantage of oral educational processes; they do not require financial or printed resources to multiply! They are not dependent on educational resources! Furthermore, without raising finances or storing and delivering printed inventory, those in hostile areas are able to be more discrete and not draw attention to themselves.

Chapter 7

The Influence of Restricting Movement Growth

GROUP SUPPORT FROM PERSONAL relationships increases the likelihood for creating a new movement. The mechanics for creating groups is dependent on new believers rapidly and enthusiastically sharing what they just learned (such as a transformative bible story) with their personal network of friends. But obstacles may arise.

One obstacle that limits or stops sharing happens if new converts don't yet realize they are immediately qualified to share. Part of the response to this dilemma was discussed in chapter 5 by emphasizing the new believer's level of required knowledge for evangelism and discipleship is within the bible story they tell and not in them. Relying on stories as the curriculum source for knowledge is sufficient to qualify rather than relying on sufficient theological knowledge. But new believers must be encouraged by the persons who first told them the stories that they are now qualified to repeat the story. All they need is within the story and through the Holy Spirit and not out of their own abilities. There will come a time when preparation and study will lead to the expansion of their ministries but, until that time comes, share the stories that are known.

Encouraging new converts to immediately share Bible stories with their friends engages the new believer's natural desire to be involved in telling others and provides a model of expansion for generations to come. Consider how Jesus quickly mobilized his disciples to tell others about what he was doing despite their own weaknesses in truly understanding him theologically. Jesus' only expectations of the disciples was that they believe, obey, and tell others.

Connecting with Friends in Relational Networks

Jesus presented his initial evangelism strategy to his disciples just before sending them out to preach about the kingdom. He told them,

> Whatever house you enter, first say, "Peace be to this house." If a man of peace is there, your peace will rest upon him; but if not, it will return to you. Stay in that house, eating and drinking what they give you; for the laborer is worthy of his wages. Do not keep moving from house to house. (Luke 10:5–7)

Why did Jesus tell his disciples to "stay in that house" and "do not keep moving"? What strategic purposes motivated Jesus to give that directive? Was there more to his statement than receiving compensation as a laborer through eating and drinking in the same house? Traveling prophets and disciples were, as a cultural courtesy and practice of hospitality, often fed and housed. But Jesus emphasized they were not to continue to travel, but to remain in the home of the person of peace. Why? Staying in the home presents the opportunity to meet the person of peace's network of friends. Jesus' strategy appears to be entering into existing relationship networks as quickly as possible. The disciples were to meet and enter into *the other person's* relational networks rather than introduce them to *their* personal network. The friends of the person of peace trust their friend; they feel safe and comfortable to meet new friends in a familiar environment to them.

Another example of entering existing networks is seen after Jesus called Levi (Matthew). Jesus joined a large reception *at Levi's home* that was filled with Levi's existing network of friends (Luke 5:27–30; Mark 2:14–16), causing the Pharisees and scribes to complain to Jesus, "Why do you eat and drink with the tax collectors and sinners?" That was Jesus' strategy: be introduced by persons of peace and then to their existing relational networks.

Compare Jesus' strategy with current practices of inviting people to *our* church or *our* home network of believing friends. In fact, in books and strategies assimilating visitors into *our* existing church network of friends is often presented as a strategic ideal. But an assimilation strategy can create outcomes counterproductive to multiplying new believers.

Too often, a new believer rapidly makes so many new Christian friends and becomes involved in so many church activities (assimilation) that former friendships dissolve because they become secondary to the new Christian relationships. Finally, the new believer has become "mature" but discovers he only still knows few, if any, unbelievers. Then church members are rallied to evangelistic outreaches through a series of creative, though perhaps unnatural, activities or "cold introductions" at shopping malls and neighborhoods instead of through natural, existing relationships.

Consider the reaction of the demon-possessed man, named Legion by the demons because there were so many demons within the man. After Jesus cast out the demons, he was asked by the townspeople to leave their region. As Jesus got into the boat to depart, ". . . the man who had been demon-possessed was imploring Him that He might accompany Him." That would be an understandable response after watching his village's self-centered response to his deliverance coupled with his overwhelming gratitude to Jesus. But Jesus wouldn't permit him to join his network, but rather sent him back to tell his testimony and introduce Jesus to the man's network, saying, "go home to your people and report to them what great things the Lord has done for you, and how He had mercy on you; And he went away and began to proclaim in Decapolis what great things Jesus had done for him; and everyone was amazed" (Mark 5:1–20). Jesus clearly revealed that his strategy was not to recruit a larger company for himself, but for people to introduce his name and his works to their own relational networks.

The Apostle Peter reminded the new churches in several Asian provinces about their former personal friendships—though engaged in sinful practices (would anything else be expected?) when he wrote them: "For the time already past is sufficient for you to have carried out the desire of the Gentiles, having pursued a course of sensuality, lusts, drunkenness, carousing, drinking parties and abominable idolatries" (1 Pet 4:3). Apart from their sinful excesses, their valuable relationships needed to be kept and redeemed, if possible, rather than automatically rejected and forgotten. Peter described the likely reactions of these former friends to their new Christian lifestyle when he wrote, "In all this, they are surprised that you do not run with them into the same excesses of dissipation and they malign you" (1 Pet 4:4). Peter continued to encourage these believers experiencing intimidation from their friends by writing, ". . . even if you should suffer for the sake of righteousness, you are blessed. And do not fear their intimidation, and do not be troubled, but sanctify Christ as Lord in your hearts, always being ready to make a defense to everyone who asks you to give an account for the hope that is in you, yet with gentleness and reverence" (1 Pet 3:14–15). Jesus didn't promote isolating and leaving former friends, but rather for the person of peace to become the entry point for his light and love to enter into a new network of friends.

So the process begins by first identifying the persons of peace—the critical entry point person into a new cultural network of relationships. This relational network is preferably left intact so that the members are introduced to Jesus through their old friend but new believer. These new believers transform their relationships to a new faith-centric relational network that explores living out a biblical worldview together to sustain, protect, encourage, love, and exhort one another. As this new faith community enlarges, its members begin introducing Jesus to other networks to which they belong, which become new entry points to those other networks. That's how multiplication is supposed to work.

Steve Addison identifies this process as a movement: "Movements are social organisms more than they are organizations; their organizing structure is formed by overlapping networks of relationships."[1] Addison further identifies the process of conversion growth through friendships in these networks according to sociological research:

> Conversion is a social phenomenon; it is often about accepting the faith of one's friends. Whatever someone's prior beliefs, he is far more likely to adopt a new faith if he witnesses a friend or family member convert to that faith. As the number of recently converted friends and family increases, so does the likelihood of conversion.
>
> As open movements grow, their "social surface" expands exponentially. Each new member opens up new networks of relationships between the movement and potential members. For continued exponential growth, a movement must maintain such open relationships with outsiders, and it must also reach out into new, adjacent social networks. Contagious relationships are at the heart of the spread of every movement; when new religious movements become closed social networks, they fail.
>
> Early Christianity grew because converts maintained open relationships with the social worlds from which they came. If the church had responded to persecution and ridicule by becoming a closed, secretive sect, there is no way it could have continued to win new converts.[2]

Preserving existing relationships and introducing Jesus to friends before those relationships and networks dissolve creates a critical time frame

---

1. Addison, *Movements that Change the World*, Kindle 1066–67.
2. Addison, *Movements that Change the World*, Kindle 989–99.

for sharing opportunities for the new believer. Only the new believer can initiate this process because only the new believer is *within* the network.

The next step for new believers is to ensure they are equipped and "able to teach others also." The answer on how to equip them has more to do with our definition of ability: is it ability to communicate or ability to transfer quantities of theological content? If it is the latter, then the process demands more time to allow the believer to learn the content—time that extends the critical time frame and jeopardizes the benefits of reaching personal relationships quickly. If it is the former, then all that is required is the confidence to tell a personal testimony and at least one story introducing Jesus from the Bible—perhaps the story that influenced him or her to come to faith. Being able to tell stories immediately allows for the process of a movement to move quickly through the community and allows for the expansion of corroborating testimonies and stories of faith from a growing number of new believers.

How does a movement grow among first-generation new believers using generational reproduction? Consider the experience of Jesus' encounter with the Samaritan woman at Jacob's well in Samaria (John 4:5–30). Jesus revealed his awareness of her multiple marriages and her current relationship and revealed that he was the Messiah. She left Jesus to tell her testimony and her growing opinion that Jesus might actually be the Messiah to her village network: "Come, see a man who told me all the things that I have done; this is not the Christ, is it?" (v. 29). The villagers' response to this introduction was to come out to meet Jesus.

What was the extent of this woman's theological understanding? It was limited to two stories: her interaction with Jesus and Jesus' revelation that he was the Messiah. But that was sufficient because ". . . many of the Samaritans believed in Him because of the word of the woman who testified, 'He told me all the things that I have done'" (John 4:39). It was enough for them to want to know more about Jesus and so they invited Jesus to stay for two days. That led to "Many more believed because of *His* word and they were saying to the woman, "It is no longer because of what *you* said that we believe, for we have heard for ourselves and know that this One is indeed the Savior of the world" (John 4:41–42, emphasis added).

The Samaritans' faith obviously matured and became personally appropriated, but it began with one woman's limited testimony that significantly multiplied throughout the village. She was the person of peace who introduced Jesus to the Samaritans through her personal relational network of friends. She was the second generation—the "convert"—who possessed the ability to teach others also with her story, bringing people to believe in Jesus after which the Lord continued to mature their personal faith.

Creating a Movement

Different disciplines understand and define movements according to their own discipline's unique perspectives. In church planting literature, a movement is often defined by the presence of at least four generations of churches. In sociological literature, it's common for us to discuss movements such as the civil rights movement in America. But when and how do movements happen? Critical dynamics can either trigger movements or strangle them. Addison presents five keys to spreading the gospel through movements:

> *White-hot faith.* Movements that change the world may eventually come to possess resources, learning and power, but they do not begin with these things. Missionary movements begin with men and women who encounter the living God and surrender in loving obedience to his call.
> *Commitment to a cause.* A movement emerges when people commit to a cause. People who change the world live in alignment with their deeply held beliefs. A movement ceases to exist when no one cares anymore.
> *Contagious relationships.* When movements spread rapidly, they do so through preexisting networks of relationships. Networks of relationships are the means by which a movement expands. They also provide the building blocks that give a movement its strength.
> *Rapid mobilization.* They won new converts and recruited fresh workers wherever they traveled. None of this was centrally planned, funded or controlled.
> Missionary movements spread through the efforts of ordinary people. The rapid spread of the gospel requires the efforts of non-professionals who are not dependent on external funding and are not strictly controlled. Converts immediately begin sharing their faith and making disciples. Key leaders model effective ministry;[3]

Two easily identifiable characteristics define a movement:

---

3. Addison, *Movements that Change the World*, Kindle 225–44.

1. It is more than a one-time event or initiative.
2. It possesses the ability to be self-perpetuating, creating generations.

For example, if you held a powerful evangelistic outreach resulting in hundreds of conversions, it would not qualify as a movement. If you scheduled the same evangelistic initiative year after year, that would still not be a self-perpetuating movement; it is simply a series of repeated one-time events. A movement must be an event that, within itself, perpetuates itself for generations.

The movement, unlike the evangelistic outreaches, is not dependent upon *your* initiative but upon what develops and organizes *from within* the new believers' community and resources. To trigger and sustain a movement requires an awareness of the sociological dynamics at play.

Movements possess:

1. a social structure comprising members with both strong and weak ties, and
2. a culture, bringing conformity to values and behaviors that provides group identity that are supported through peer pressure.

Strong ties are sociologists' description of those who have direct relationships with the influencers, initiators, and leaders of the movement. Weak ties describe those who identify with the movement and have a personal relationship with others in the movement but have no direct relationship with the movement's leaders. The powerful influence of weak ties was identified in the late 1960s by Mark Granovetter.

> When sociologists have examined how opinions move through communities, how gossip spreads or political movements start, they've discovered a common pattern: Our weak-tie acquaintances are often as influential—if not more—than our close-tie friends. As Granovetter wrote, "Individuals with few weak ties will be deprived of information from distant parts of the social system and will be confined to the provincial news and views of their close friends . . . While members of one or two cliques may be efficiently recruited, the problem is that, without weak ties, any momentum generated in this way does not spread beyond the clique. As a result, most of the population will be untouched.[4]

---

4. Duhigg, *Power of Habit*, Kindle 3454; citing Granovetter, "The Strength of Weak Ties: A Network Theory Revisited," *Sociological Theory* 1 (1983) 201–33.

Weak ties characterize spiritual generations who may likely never meet the person who first generated their spiritual lineage. But weak ties provide critical and essential benefits to the movement. They provide peer pressure that often spreads broadly through extended networks. A broad network of weak ties has access to very different sources of information that can provide early alerts of danger from the majority culture. Weak ties explain how a few people protesting something can quickly grow into a broad movement.

Multiplication is proposed as an effective remedy to counteract the weaknesses associated with addition. Similarly, movements grown by overlapping networks of relationships is proposed as an effective strategy to maximize multiplication within networks. But movements are also subject to negative influences that can limit or even terminate their continuation.

Negative Influences Affecting Movement Strategy

Roland Allen was an Anglican priest ordained at age twenty-five in 1893. He served many years in China—at one point overseeing six provinces for the Anglican's Society for the Propagation of the Gospel. He also ministered in India and Africa before dying in Nairobi, Kenya in 1947. He thought deeply about the challenge of establishing indigenous churches based upon the Apostle Paul's missionary methods and recorded his conclusions by writing ten books—among which was *The Spontaneous Expansion of the Church, and the Causes That Hinder It*. Allen defined spontaneous expansion as

> . . . the expansion which follows the unexhorted and unorganized activity of individual members of the Church explaining to others the Gospel which they have found for themselves. . .
>
> Spontaneous expansion begins with the individual effort of the individual Christian to assist his fellow, when common experience, common difficulties, common toil have first brought the two together. It is this equality and community of experience which makes the one deliver his message in terms which the other can understand, and makes the hearer approach the subject with sympathy and confidence--with sympathy because the common experience makes approach easy and natural, with confidence, because the one is accustomed to understand what the other says and expects to understand him now.[5]

---

5. Allen, *Spontaneous Expansion of the Church*, Kindle 110, 153–57.

Part 2: Countering Negative Influences

The goals and the processes of spontaneous expansion described by Allen in 1927 align with our contemporary description of movements. His observations and suggestions are clearly relevant to this discussion. Steve Addison provides an excellent simplified summary of Allen's book:

> According to Allen, spontaneous expansion is *inhibited* under these conditions:
>
> 1. When paid foreign professionals are primarily responsible to spread the gospel, causing the gospel to be seen as an alien intrusion.
> 2. When the church is dependent on foreign funds and leadership. Allen asked, "How can a man propagate a religion which he cannot support and which he cannot expect those whom he addresses to be able to support?"
> 3. When the spread of the gospel is controlled out of fear of error, and both error and godly zeal are suppressed.
> 4. When it is believed that the church is to be founded, educated, equipped and established in the doctrine, ethics and organization before it is to expand.
> 5. When emerging leaders are restricted from ministering until they are fully trained and so learn the lesson of inactivity and dependency.
> 6. When conversion is seen as the result of clever argument rather than the power of Christ.
> 7. When professional clergy control the ministry and discourage the spontaneous zeal of nonprofessionals. They may protect the new believers from charlatans like Simon the magician (Acts 8: 9–24), but in doing so they also block unconventional leaders like Peter the fisherman.
>
> According to Allen, spontaneous expansion is *enhanced* under these conditions:
>
> 1. When new converts *immediately* (*emphasis* added) tell their story to those who know them.
> 2. When, from the beginning, evangelism is the work of those within the culture.
> 3. When true doctrine results from the true experience of the power of Christ rather than mere intellectual instruction. Heresies are not produced by ignorance but by the speculations of learned men.
> 4. When the church is self-supporting and provides for its own leaders and facilities.

5. When new churches are given the freedom to learn by experience and are supported but not controlled. Allen believed the great things of God are beyond human control. He observed that control produces sterility. Controlled converts may not go astray, but they produce nothing.[6]

First in both lists of what inhibits and what enhances spontaneous expansion is the strategic practice of new converts immediately telling friends rather than waiting for and relying upon "professional" clergy or missionaries. With such a large task and responsibility to witness to an overwhelming population, Allen recognized that the task of multiplication relying upon the first native believers to begin their own spiritual generations was the only viable strategy.

> Many years ago my experience in China taught me that if our object was to establish in that country a Church that might spread over the six provinces that then formed the diocese of North China, that object could only be attained if the first Christians who were converted by our labours understood clearly that they could by themselves, without any further assistance from us, not only convert their neighbours, but establish Churches. That meant that the very first groups of converts must be so fully equipped with all spiritual authority that they could multiply themselves without any necessary reference to us: that, though, while we were there, they might regard us as helpful advisers, yet our removal should not at all mutilate the completeness of the Church, or deprive it of anything necessary for its unlimited expansion.[7]

Allen described the difficulty he faced from missionary colleagues who would not trust new believers to initiate spontaneous evangelism apart from the governance of mature supervising leaders or elders. To trust new believers to spread rapidly as weak ties, as described earlier, led his colleagues to be fearful of the loss of control. As Allen interpreted the concern,

> We fear it because we feel that it is something that we cannot control. And that is true. We can neither induce nor control spontaneous expansion whether we look on it as the work of the individual or of the Church, simply because it is spontaneous . . .

---

6. Addison, *Movements that Change the World*, Kindle 1254–76.
7. Allen, *Spontaneous Expansion of the Church*, Kindle 13–19.

we instinctively think of something which we cannot control as tending to disorder.⁸

Allen therefore provides two options: allow new believers to reach others unrelated directly to the established leadership (weak ties of the movement), which will produce spontaneous expansion, or retain established leadership control, which will terminate the potential for spontaneous expansion.

Allen's recognition that the task "could *only* be attained" (emphasis added) by emphasizing "that they could by themselves, without any further assistance from us" is an additional confirmation that multiplication requires replacement as described in the previous chapter. But notice the second requirement: "the very first groups of converts must be so fully equipped with all spiritual authority that they could multiply themselves."

Why Storytelling Is a Remedy

An emphasis in chapter 3 was that spiritual authority resides in the story and not the storyteller. The storyteller is the facilitator and, rather than being the authoritative spiritual source, tells the biblical story, which is truly the authoritative source. It is the access to biblical stories that fully equips a believer!

New believers can tell at least two stories immediately after committing their faith in Christ: the story of their testimony and a biblical story of Jesus that caused them to believe in him as Savior. There may be no other information available to them at that point; there is little teaching new believers can do or be responsible to know. That's the extent of their status of being "fully equipped," but that is all that can and should be required of a new believer. When Jesus healed the man born blind, the Pharisees questioned the man theologically. At first, the man made a theological determination: he called Jesus a prophet (John 9:17). But that was an insufficient answer to the Pharisees, who thought Jesus did not meet the theological criteria because he healed on the Sabbath. They wanted the man to conclude with them that Jesus was a sinner. The man wasn't equipped to argue with these theological elites; he could only reply, "Whether He is a sinner, I do not know; one thing I do know, that though I was blind, now I see" (John 9:25). That's sufficient information for a new believer to communicate to a friend.

---

8. Allen, *Spontaneous Expansion of the Church*, Kindle 190–92, 213–14.

The Influence of Restricting Movement Growth

Allen's missionary associates believed more teaching was required through professional clergy or missionaries to ensure the movement's continuation.

> It is hindered by a very widespread conviction amongst our missionaries that new converts, so far from evangelizing others, need to be nursed themselves if they are not to fall away. We often hear some such expression as this: "Even after baptism the new life in Christ must be carefully tended or inevitably the first fervor will cool and the early enthusiasm will be quenched by the deadly heathenism all round." That is a voice with which we are very familiar, which teaches that the way to retain the consciousness of a gift received is not by handing it on to others, but by learning to depend more and more on teachers; and that it is our wisdom to expect nothing from our converts, but to watch over them and nurse them and feed them. It is a voice which appeals more and more insistently for paid and trained workers to guard and to protect a life which must otherwise inevitably be quenched . . . It is hindered by a very widespread conviction that we cannot trust untrained men to propagate the Faith.[9]

Telling biblical stories does not require theological training that delays a new believer from sharing with friends. Telling biblical stories allows and encourages new believers to express their natural desire to share their faith with other friends. The initial telling of a biblical story models the entire process of sharing with another without requiring advanced teaching first. Encouraging each generation to reach other friends in overlapping relational networks enables the movement to begin as an indigenous movement that quickly spreads.

How can stories extend broadly and quickly by untrained new believers? There is often a sense of righteous restraint and the need for permission from theological leaders to minister in a controlled manner. Allen continues,

> Nor is there any doubt what the restraining influence is. It is fear for the doctrine. He is afraid that the doctrine may be misrepresented by the unguided zeal of native Christians to teach others what they have learned. I do not think he is afraid that his converts would willfully and deliberately misrepresent it: I think that he rather doubts their knowledge of it, and their ability to express it as he thinks that it ought to be expressed. This fear compels him

---

9. Allen, *Spontaneous Expansion of the Church*, Kindle 50–512.

to say that we cannot possibly permit native Christians to express their spontaneous zeal in teaching others what they have learned, and in so saying he proclaims that we can generally restrain it, and do so. He proclaims also that, if we did not restrain it, spontaneous zeal would in fact spread the knowledge of the doctrine far and wide.[10]

The fear that "cannot allow" and "cannot permit" new believers to tell biblical stories results from the conviction that doctrine must be defended with all vigilance not only for ourselves but for all who learn to believe on Christ through our preaching. With that responsibility comes a belief that Scripture can be misrepresented except by the most mature.[11] But telling stories accurately doesn't involve theologizing and defining "in-house" theological arguments. Storytelling is the purest way to communicate Scripture, leaving Scripture itself as the authority. Limiting theological discussions to the content of biblical stories—that is, "what does the story say?"—provides sufficient safety for new believers to avoid theological conjectures or processes that can lead to heresies.

Preferring this initial biblical theology approach over a systematic theology approach limits the dangers of applying preconceived meanings to the stories that often develop from questions that come from the narrow or misconstrued worldviews discussed in chapter 4. Emphasizing what the story *says* rather than explaining what the story *means* keeps the authority with the biblical story and protects both the story and the storyteller. Indeed, all seven negative influences identified by Roland Allen and the criticisms and fears of trusting new believers can be resolved, or at least addressed, through dependence on storytelling.

But the overall goal is not just to encourage growth by applying movement theory to multiplying storytellers, but rather to prepare for the kingdom of God by impacting our world through the church. Such impact cannot happen if the movement doesn't mature and develop faith communities or if new believers do not remain unified in community. Allowing new believers to remain independent from the new community or church is the next (and sixth) negative influence, and storytelling has a role to play in establishing a community strategy as discussed in the next chapter.

---

10. Allen *Spontaneous Expansion of the Church*, Kindle 679–85.
11. Allen, *Spontaneous Expansion of the Church*, Kindle 693–95.

Chapter Summary

The person of peace is an influential member of a network of friends who welcomes the opportunity to be introduced to Jesus Christ. This person also welcomes the opportunity to introduce Jesus to his or her friends within their relational network. The introduction is uncomplicated, merely requiring telling a story about how the interest or belief affected them personally and a biblical story about Jesus that the person had heard. There is no pressure on the person because the person is only facilitating a discussion about the stories and not teaching about Jesus or Christianity.

These introductions move through the network of friends who have overlapping networks of their own. Some of them will naturally assume the role of persons of peace to their friends in other networks. When Jesus is introduced to these overlapping networks, a movement is begun. Movements possess a social structure of both strong and weak relationships among the people, both of which are essential for its growth and safety. Shared values and behaviors unite these people, which forms a new culture that gives the movement its identity.

Negative and positive influences can inhibit, terminate, or enhance these faith movements to grow. The most critical influence is the first generation believers or evangelists, who must ensure the next-generation converts possess the ability to teach others by faithfully and quickly introducing Jesus to their relational networks before their relational networks weaken or dissolve. This relational sharing cannot be delayed by waiting for deeper theological preparation or interfered with by introducing other missionaries who are foreign to their networks. Instead, new believers are immediately able to tell their own testimony and at least one biblical story for discussion. This is the remedy to ensure a movement's success because telling stories provides the best assurance for safety and eliminates any hindrance from a lack of Christian literature or resources (financial or trained personnel).

Chapter 8

The Influence of Diverse Beliefs and Practices within The Community

WHEREAS THE PREVIOUS CHAPTER presented personal relationships as the foundational *social structure* of a movement, this chapter presents influences affecting the *culture* of a movement. Storytelling impacts and is impacted by both the structure and the culture as new storytelling communities of faith are formed. Corinth is our case study.

Corinth was a large, influential, and wealthy city on the isthmus connecting Greece to the Peloponnese. The Apostle Peter was the first evangelist to visit Corinth, evidently penetrating a household community with the gospel and establishing it as a faith community before continuing his trip to Rome. After Peter departed, a zealous Alexandrian, Apollos, arrived and continued evangelizing among the Corinthians. While Apollos continued his ministry, the Apostle Paul arrived with his team and also began evangelizing and penetrating other new households of faith. These overlapping networks of relational communities—and others such as one led by Chloe—had the potential of forming a larger Christian movement that could spread and impact the entire region. Paul departed, expecting these communities to continue their growth and influence together, but soon received word that the movement was fracturing in disunity. Paul wrote to them,

> For I have been informed concerning you, my brethren, by Chloe's people, that there are quarrels among you. Now I mean this, that each one of you is saying, "I am of Paul," and "I of Apollos," and "I of Peter," and "I of Christ." Has Christ been divided? (1 Cor 1:11–13)

Influence of Diverse Beliefs and Practices

The sixth potential negative influence limiting spiritual reproduction is exposed when the community relationships weaken, fracture, and potentially end due to different visions, different ministry practices, or different methods of teaching and building disciples. The first correction Paul offered the Corinthians was to return to a spirit of humility and equality of service under Christ and the Holy Spirit (1 Cor 1:13—2:5). Such an attitude adjustment was foundational.

But, additional to a renewed commitment to humility and unity, there are behaviors that must be developed for any movement to continue to reproduce. Research indicates 40 percent of our daily behaviors are not initiated by actual decisions but by habits developed through repetition.[1] Therefore, to see lives change, we must address intentional change from old habits to new—habitual behaviors that are reflected in biblical stories. Personal habits coupled with public habits encourages mutual accountability and results in people moving forward together while developing and modeling a distinctive cultural form to their faith community.

The healthiest mission agencies and churches have strong cultures because their members agree to maintain the same vision, attitudes, and discipleship practices, and to hold each other accountable to their vision and process. Without a culture, there is no sense of belonging, identity, or allegiance to the emerging community. Without a culture, there is peril because personal accountability or protection of the person is lacking. Without a culture, the impact of the movement becomes indistinguishable from the majority culture. A movement needs a culture that can be positively influenced by biblical storying, which results in assuring the stories remain unchanging and truthful in the telling. Every oral culture relies on the members to ensure the oral histories, vision, and values are told and retold accurately. Similarly, biblical stories must be reviewed by the movement's storying community to ensure accuracy through the generations. The faith community needs the oral stories to create their identity and define their culture and the oral storytellers need a strong, unified, and healthy faith community to ensure the stories are told accurately throughout spiritual generations.

---

1. Duhigg, *Power of Habit*, Kindle 119.

Part 2 : Countering Negative Influences

Developing Spiritual Habits

Spiritual practices, or disciplines, are habits that, through practice, intention, and habitual repetition produce a changed life. The discipler/mentor must teach these disciplines to the new believer and assist in developing them. Teaching these disciplines can be taught through well-designed biblical story lessons.

Many spiritual practices, such as meditation or prayer, are practiced using different intentions and purposes by non-Christian religions. Therefore, the storyteller must select transformative stories that reform the misconceptions and practices so they are built upon biblical foundations. Whereas other religions often apply these disciplines to earn God's favor through a sense of duty or obedience or for self-improvement, Christian foundations build upon a loving, personal relationship with God, whose acceptance and approval was already given through Jesus Christ's work on the cross.

The faith community's encouragement of spiritual habits comes from modeling public community practices and through accountability of close relationships. *Personal habits* with accountability and *public habits* with modeling are powerful influencers that shape lives and strengthen the communities' unity. A stronger community provides a check on stories to ensure their accuracy through spiritual generations of storytellers.

Develop Community Culture through Community Habits

A common suspicion about relying on the integrity of stories is that they inevitably undergo change in the process of retelling and are therefore undependable to strengthen communities. The concern about inevitable change to the story is usually voiced among people from literate societies but not heard among those from oral societies. Oral societies know that without absolute accuracy telling their history from one generation to another, their people would lose their history and therefore their community and place in the world.

Therefore, oral societies practice telling stories to each other in their communities and require their children to learn their own genealogy and values from an early age. Learning the same story, each member of the community assumes the role of self-correcting and self-protecting the integrity of their shared history. They practice telling their stories with each other to

Influence of Diverse Beliefs and Practices

ensure accuracy and uniformity of the story. Christian communities must practice this behavior! A culture is strengthened by its public habits of reviewing stories together, which also assures the correction of any errors as the communities are constantly self-correcting.

Using stories to reinforce values, heritage, and history is valuable for both oral and literate cultures. Sometime, an older and more literate generation expresses astonishment and dismay that the younger, more visually and orally focused generation is increasingly unable to answer historical questions about their family, church, community, or country's history and values. The growing ignorance can be traced to the neglect of repeating the same stories that framed and protected the identity of the national or community's values, behaviors, and cultural rituals. When the argument is voiced that the historical record was wrong, attempts are made to reinterpret or rewrite the history from the perspective of modern influences and ideals. Be aware that the stories are always under attack, whether through intentional disregard or repeated with critical changes to suit different values that replace the old story with a new one. That's the power of story; it's the glue of the community. Therefore, repeat biblical stories as an essential public and personal practice to protect the story from all contemporary influences.

Charles Duhigg offers an excellent summary of forming a movement from creating relationships and maturing based upon habits:

> A movement *starts* because of the social habits of friendship and the strong ties between close acquaintances. It *grows* because of the habits of a community, and the weak ties that hold neighborhoods and clans together. And it *endures* because a movement's leaders give participants new habits that create a fresh sense of identity and a feeling of ownership. Usually, only when all three parts of this process are fulfilled can a movement become self-propelling and reach a critical mass.[2]

A culture strengthens the community as it declares its values, habits, ministry, history, and activities. The community becomes the place of safety; the community defends each other and supports each member. One of the challenges of an older church is to ensure the children are told the history of the church's founding. Without knowing the history of the beginning church, the children don't know and respect the steps of faith and

---

2. Duhigg, *Power of Habit*, Kindle 3347, emphasis added.

challenge of the early years and lose the sight of their own value and place in the heritage of the church.

A church that has a strong community and culture is the regularity of its scheduled gatherings and life. Irregular meetings are often poorly attended because it requires a special decision to attend, which limits it becoming a habit and won't be attended except by a few. The relational structure and the habitual practices of the faith community are critical for the continuation of the movement's culture. Regularly scheduled times for story teams to meet to craft or rehearse stories are essential for the storytelling, and the stories told can reinforce the heritage, culture, and faith stories of the church for future generations.

I placed my faith in Jesus Christ as my Savior and Lord in 1971 through the ministry of The Navigators while I served in the U.S. Navy at Norfolk, Virginia. There were seventeen Navigator Bible study teams among sailors in the area during that time. Many of the team leaders lived in the same housing development and it was the practice of many of us to go to their homes on Saturday mornings to work and serve them so they could be free to minister to us during the week. Many Saturdays I was driven to that development and saw houses with ten to fifteen men who had descended on a single home trimming shrubs, mowing the lawn, painting, and all kinds of home improvement projects. Our work would then be rewarded by a homemade lunch in appreciation for our efforts. As a new Christian, I thought this was the normal Christian lifestyle and I loved it!

It was a few more years before I realized I was part of a unique culture. Other church groups did not have those practices. But during those early months, it was unthinkable *not* to go to the house on Saturday because, well, that's what we did. As a culture, our public habit helped establish inward faithfulness. If we only gathered together occasionally when required, we wouldn't have had a culture; we would only have had a workday and we would have been on our own to determine whether or not we wanted to attend. After several weeks, I was invited to leave the base on Friday night to sleep on a bunk bed in my team leader Barry and Louise's family room to have Bible study early Saturday morning before the others joined us for the home projects. The whole team enjoyed singing and socializing together. Those public habits helped me move toward faithfulness in private habits of study and worship. The schedules and activities were so established and brought such fruitfulness from so many of my friends and peers that it would be unthinkable not to participate.

Peer Pressure as Persecution or Accountability

Peer pressure develops within any social community and can be either a positive or negative influence in the growth of the community. Negative peer pressure is present when a friend attempts to convince the new believer to renounce his or her faith and return to a former lifestyle. But positive peer pressure is described in Ecclesiastes 4:9–10: "Two are better than one because they have a good return for their labor. For if either of them falls, the one will lift up his companion. But woe to the one who falls when there is not another to lift him up."

The writer of Hebrews addressed positive peer pressure and encouragement for the new churches when he wrote, "... and let us consider how to stimulate one another to love and good deeds, not forsaking our own assembling together, as is the habit of some, but encouraging one another ... " (Heb 10:24–25). That is a clear call to ensure the culture of the church includes mutual accountability and encouragement. This faith community's expression of kindly peer pressure is not optional but a required element to maintain a movement.

A society's majority culture is confident in its power as it relies on its size and history to support its values and beliefs by applying different forms of pressure throughout all levels of society. However, a minority Christian movement can survive the influence of the majority culture by enforcing its own cultural strength internally through both the strong and the weak relational ties within the community. The enlarged number of weak ties enforces the will of the majority culture through the use of peer pressure. It's a form of persuasion that has been remarkably effective over many centuries. It's the sense of obligation that neighborhoods or communities place upon themselves. In other words, peer pressure.

Peer pressure—and the social habits that encourage people to conform to group expectations—is difficult to describe, because it often differs in form and expression from person to person. These social habits aren't as much one consistent pattern as dozens of individual habits that ultimately cause everyone to move in the same direction.

David DeSilva understands the motivation and the manner of peer pressure, identifying shaming as a tool of peer pressure used by the majority culture. It is used to rescue and restore people to live in conformity with their cultural values and to protect itself from the potential of more people withdrawing from the community to join the emerging minority culture. But this very same application of peer pressure can also be applied among the members of the minority culture to resist the majority culture peer pressure.

> The references to society's attempts to pressure the Christian "deviants" back into conformity with Greco-Roman or traditional Jewish values could be multiplied indefinitely. It is noteworthy that maligning, reproach, beatings, imprisonments and financial ruin are mentioned frequently and explicitly, but lynching or execution only rarely: their neighbors were trying to reclaim these wayward members of their society.[3]

From this perspective, what is viewed by one side as persecution is viewed by the other side as upholding and defending the communities' beliefs, values, and practices to maintain its cultural stability. The relationship between the two perspectives does not legitimize the purpose for persecution; that's a different issue. Jesus was shamed as he was viewed as a threat to the cultural institutions of the Torah, the Sabbath, the temple, and the priestly power structure—but he was legitimate in doing so when he confronted the illegitimate use of those institutions!

Establishing new communities of faith are essential for a movement to develop because they provide an identity and protection for the new believer. Also essential for new believers to resist shaming is to hear stories about how the first disciples and apostles faced and overcame the shame and persecution that believers historically face. They need to hear the authority of biblical stories told consistently within the faith community. They need to hear and tell stories that give understanding how the first century believers resisted and coped with the pressures of their friends. They need to identify with those who suffered shame but were ultimately victorious and honored, and that identification comes from well-chosen stories.

Death on a cross was the ultimate expression of shame. Yet, the author of Hebrews wrote about Jesus, ". . . who for the joy set before Him, endured the cross, despising the shame, and has sat down at the right hand of the throne of God" (Heb 12:2). The Apostle Peter (1 Pet 2:7) drew on the prophecy "The stone which the builders rejected has become the chief cornerstone" (Ps 118:22) to connect the path from rejection to honored cornerstone.

The shame evaluation came from the majority Jewish culture, but the apostles presented Jesus' death as honorable because it was a virtuous voluntary death that provided life and benefits to others. As Mark wrote in his

---

3. DeSilva, *Honor, Patronage, Kinship and Purity*, 45

Influence of Diverse Beliefs and Practices

gospel, "For even the Son of Man came not to be served but to serve, and to give his life a ransom for many" (Mark 10:45). After DeSilva recorded numerous scriptures attesting to the honorable life and death too lengthy to record here, he concludes, "The death of Jesus was in every respect, then, an honorable death, despite the vehicle by which it was effected. The failure on the part of the world to understand this fact speaks of their ignorance, not Jesus' degradation."[4] New believers, exposed to stories and teachings through their new Christian culture, reinforce the honor of Jesus and resist the maligning of those who disparage both Jesus and his followers. The New Testament authors resisted being maligned by dismissing those enemies of the cross as ignorant and wicked, such as Paul's descriptions to the Ephesian church:

> So this I say and affirm together with the Lord; that you walk no longer just as the Gentiles also walk, in the futility of their mind, being darkened in their understanding, excluded from the life of God because of the ignorance that is in them, because of the hardness of their heart; and they, having become callous, have given themselves over to sensuality for the practice of every kind of impurity with greediness." (Eph 4:17–19)

The purpose of these descriptions, according to DeSilva, is not to make a theological point based upon the enemies' character. Instead, the purpose is to strengthen the resolve of the believers by identifying the enemies' inability to form a reliable evaluation of worth and reveal their utter shamelessness in the light of God's revelation of God's standards. To be shamed by the shameless is ultimately no shame at all. In fact, contemplating the vice of their detractors transforms their own experience of rejection into a sign of their honor.[5]

Ultimately, vindication against the enemies' persecutions is answered by learning about God's day of judgement, when God will judge those who reject his Son. This serves as motivation against Jesus' new followers returning to their previous lifestyle to escape their former friends' persecutions and insults. Learning and telling the biblical stories of Abel, Enoch, and Noah (Hebrews 11), and particularly the stories of Abraham and Moses, provides lessons about continuing in faith and waiting to receive the better rewards of honor in the future.

---

4. DeSilva, *Honor, Patronage, Kinship and Purity*, 53.
5. DeSilva, *Honor, Patronage, Kinship and Purity*, 63.

Part 2 : Countering Negative Influences

By remaining within a strong community of believers, even the severe experiences of persecution become evidences of honor, much as Peter and the apostles expressed after their flogging by the Sanhedrin: "So they went on their way from the presence of the Council, rejoicing that they had been considered worthy to suffer shame for His name" (Acts 5:41). Such honor was also given by John when writing his letters to the seven churches of the book of Revelation.

Jesus prepared his followers for inevitable persecution (Matt 24:9; John 15:18–21) and Peter told them not to be surprised at their "fiery ordeal . . . as though some strange thing were happening to you" (1 Pet 4:12). "The experience of shaming was meant by outsiders to make the Christians feel abnormal and make them wish to retreat back into the safety of conformity. Paul, however, turns the experience of being shamed into something 'normal' for the existence of believers in the world."[6]

Though the peer pressure of the outsiders—represented by shaming, maligning, or persecution—is intended to draw the person back into the majority culture, the peer pressure of the believers is to inform, protect, motivate, and hold accountable the new believer to persevere in their commitment to Jesus. Thus the maligning of Jesus is transformed to reveal the honor of his sacrifice. Outsiders become identified as people living in darkness who are unaware of the light. The return to the previous life is redefined as dishonoring God, which will be punished on the Day of Judgment. Those who disciple new believers must teach these principles that counter the outsiders' shame and punishment, and the new believer must shift his or her primary loyalty to the new community and biblical truths. Telling stories that communicate how the shame of others becomes honorable, provides the encouragement of being part of a larger spiritual community, and is a way for new believers to encourage other new believers to live courageously and resist the negative effects of persecution.

Chapter Summary

Ensuring a new faith community continues reproducing spiritual generations requires members to be humble and unified in vision and habitual practices that establish their identity and culture. Teaching personal habits of spiritual disciplines, supported by community habits of worship, service, and devotion, strengthens the community and provides a safe environment

---

6. DeSilva. *Honor, Patronage, Kinship and Purity*, 66.

for new believers to grow in their faith. Learning how to resist forms of persecution, such as peer pressure from their former friends who wish to pull them back to their previous lifestyle, can be learned and modeled through telling biblical stories that encourage believers to resist the misconceptions of shame and recognize the strength of honor that transforms dishonor.

Bible storying groups within the community who select and craft stories according to the needs of their community provide a regular opportunity to fellowship together, study together, hold each other accountable, and develop stories together. This should be an initial and productive step in creating a strengthened community.

But the studying group also needs a strong faith community to review the stories consistently through the years to ensure that the stories do not deviate from their truths. Only as the storytellers are accountable to the community, and the community strengthened by the storytellers, will there be safety and strength for spiritual generations to come.

Chapter 9

The Influence of Leadership Using Local but Unbiblical Criteria

THE MOTHER OF JAMES and John took them with her to Jesus requesting the two be installed leaders when Jesus became king (Matt 20:20–21). This was "how things were done" and she didn't question the system; leaders were expected to be appointed by the existing authority. Existing leadership appoints and empowers only those who support and protect the existing traditions and authority. Consequently, there are few opportunities for new leaders to emerge who are not members of the inside power relationships. Therefore, an emerging Christian movement outside those relationships doesn't have access to local leadership training. Leadership training is restricted to outside observation of local leadership behaviors.

Comparing the servant leadership modeled by Jesus with local models of leadership governed by power, intimidation, and prestige reveals such striking differences of values and behaviors that they represent two competing worldviews. Jesus directly confronted the existing Roman and Jewish leadership models as a false worldview to ensure his disciples rejected that expression of leadership when he said,

> You know that the rulers of the Gentiles lord it over them, and their great men exercise authority over them. It is not so among you, but whoever wishes to become great among you shall be your servant, and whoever wishes to be first among you shall be your slave; just as the Son of Man did not come to be served, but to serve, and to give His life a ransom for many. (Matt 20:25–28)

Leadership Using Local but Unbiblical Criteria

The conceptual change teaching strategy introduced in chapter 4 is illustrated in this story. Recall that the first step to cause a new conceptual understanding is to raise the person's conception/misconception to a conscious level. How did Jesus respond to her request and raise the awareness in this case? By identifying the model of leadership (that of the Gentiles) and defining its expression as lording it over others.

For almost three years of ministry under Jesus' leadership, it didn't register with the disciples that Jesus was modeling a totally different way of leading. Why? Because they hadn't been forced to directly and objectively contrast the two worldviews until Jesus forced them to do so in this interchange. They had never been forced to make a decision for preference or rejection between the two views. Power and lordship was the model their mother was accustomed to seeing and the sons accepted it without recognizing its variance with Jesus' leadership model.

Now that the disciples' awareness of their leadership assumptions were raised to a conscious level, Jesus contrasted their current worldview with a different worldview—the second step of the conceptual change strategy. Jesus' different leadership worldview was to select leaders according to their ability to serve those they led—as if a slave to them! Now the two sons were forced to recognize the differences and make a decision about which model to prefer and which to reject—the third critical step of conceptual change teaching strategy.

Jesus made his preference clear with a command: ". . . it is not so among you," and added the truth that leadership is appointed by God, not even by Jesus himself. With that command and teaching, Jesus told them to eliminate their pre-existing leadership worldview. Jesus didn't say that it was wrong to seek to be great—his disciples would need to be great to fulfill their future responsibilities—but he corrected the method of how great leadership was chosen for his kingdom, and it wasn't according to the local criteria of transferred power. Do not miss that Jesus not only objected to the political power and influence of the Gentile leadership, but also the power and influence of the religious leaders. The values of servant leadership were not limited to a particular domain, whether secular or spiritual.

Other biblical values than servanthood likely conflict with the cultural expectations and values of the community. Some cultural values may be different expressions or interpretations of leadership practices that may find a biblical foundation; others may require refinement or communicating the concepts differently. And some of these expressions, upon closer

Part 2 : Countering Negative Influences

scrutiny, may cause a re-evaluation of our own understandings of our presumed values.

Local leadership is a critical challenge for a new church or Christian community, and the presence of misconceptions of biblical leadership must be exposed and confronted as essential for continued movement growth using godly, competent leaders. Misconceptions can be unintentionally imported from assumptions, influences, and values of foreign evangelists or disciplers in addition to those already present and active from local cultural values. Therefore, as in other areas, the storyteller must be particularly aware of the tendency to interpret Scripture in a way that fits their present personal worldview or demands leadership skills that goes beyond Scripture or the local cultural expectations.

For example, Gurnek Baines's insightful studies of multinational business leadership revealed "only 16 percent of American executives had a strength around intellectual flexibility compared with averages of 30–40 percent for most other cultures."[1] American leaders are simply used to—and sometimes demanding of—stable environments to plan their work and work their plan with the expectation of predictability in their environments. The highest score for flexible leadership planning in the world is held by African leaders, with 42 percent, who often live and minister in extremely unstable situations. Predictably, among those leading in such unstable environments, Baines's research revealed African leaders had the highest global need, at 49 percent, to learn to develop long-term strategic thinking; only 17 percent of African leaders were considered strong in the area of strategic thinking.[2] Though strategic planning might be a significant skill among American leadership, flexibility would be more significant in unstable or hostile environments.

Cultural expectations for leadership skills among Asian people is more focused on the values of hierarchy, harmony, and honor. Westerners tend to be more individualistic, seeking efficiency and placing high value on critical thinking. These values are largely so much a part of the culture that locals may not be aware of them; "this is just how it's done." Awareness of the value will often come from someone outside the culture who can compare the values. An East Asian person may never classify himself or herself as "collectivistic." However, the outsider status of the missionary

---

1. Baines, *Cultural DNA*, Kindle 1211–18.
2. Baines, *Cultural DNA*, Kindle 1984.

affords a perspective with more objectivity (relative to the insider), contributing to a well-rounded exchange.[3]

Leadership expectations of the home culture should not, however, be the default and defining approach when moving into the new worldviews. Christian leadership must reflect Christian values defined by Scripture. When choosing biblical stories to teach leaders, give priority to leadership qualities, but also be sensitive to the cultural expectations in the community and the influences of culture within the biblical story.

The Apostle Paul understood challenging existing expressions of leadership when he responded to Titus on the island of Crete. We aren't told about the beginnings of the Christian community. Some suggest it was through Cretans who witnessed Pentecost and returned home from Jerusalem. Others suggest Paul led many to faith as he swept through the island on an evangelistic trip. But Paul directed Titus to appoint elder leadership in Crete (Titus 1:5). It probably was not long before Titus apparently sent a message back to Paul that no one was capable of leading the church. You can almost hear his frustrated cry to Paul, "Don't you realize that all that is here are a bunch of Cretans?!"

Paul's answer was to begin the process of teaching leaders by identifying those who led their own families well—and then he offered his list of character criteria. Certainly, they had responsibility to ensure doctrine was correctly taught and incorrect teaching would be cast aside. Leadership development must start someplace and Paul suggested looking at those who could lead their family responsibly.

The Cretans certainly had their own understanding and practice of leadership—society required it—but Titus resisted their installation as leaders within the church. Instead there had to be a reforming of the nature of leadership according to Christian values; he couldn't begin a church movement on Crete relying on Cretan models of leadership.

Storytelling and Leadership Development

To develop leaders emerging as a first generation calls for the same remedy—tell stories that are simple, short, and easily reproducible, but selecting stories that illustrate leadership and character principles. Using the same storytelling lesson format for evangelism, discipleship, and leadership objectives has many benefits. It reinforces the learning process of listening

---

3. Wu. *Saving God's Face*, Kindle 1138–43.

carefully to a story and—through discussion with friends—identifies similar and relevant application points between the biblical culture and their own. Using this format reinforces the learning process, looking at stories from the perspective of discovering teaching principles rather than being entertained by a good story. Creating and telling stories that illustrate both positive and negative illustrations of leadership practices creates good discovery and discussion for a new generation of leaders to incorporate biblical principle that fit their own culture.

Not to be overlooked is that using biblical stories is a non-confrontational way to identify issues without categorizing the listeners as being trained in leadership prematurely. Also, the process of dialogue creates the opportunities for both the storyteller and the listener to uncover worldview biases previously unrecognized. New believers begin to learn biblical leadership principles immediately as they experience God's guidance and the Holy Spirit grants experiences that built faith and trust in God, such as when David justified his readiness when choosing to confront Goliath.

> When a lion or bear came and took a lamb from the flock, I went out after him and attacked him, and rescued it from his mouth; and when he rose up against me, I seized him by his beard and struck him and killed him. Your servant has killed both the lion and the bear; and this uncircumcised Philistine will be like one of them, since he has taunted the armies of the living God. And David said, "The Lord who delivered me from the paw of the lion and from the paw of the bear, He will deliver me from the hand of this Philistine." (1 Sam 17:34–37)

David learned courage and dependence on God to deliver him as he had in the past—the greatest lesson a leader could receive.

Sometimes, ministry leaders are appointed before they are recognized as prepared by God. This was the case of James, John, and their mother. Leadership appointment without evaluation of character was painfully described in the story of Eli the priest, whose sons were "worthless men; they did not know the Lord" (1 Sam 2:12) and they dishonored God. The Lord, through an unnamed man of God, prophesied that his two sons—who did evil at the tent of meeting—would die on the same day (1 Sam 2:34). Then God raised up a faithful priest to replace Eli and his sons. Samuel was then confirmed—not appointed—by all the people (1 Sam 3:20). But though Samuel faithfully judged Israel all the days of his life (1 Sam 7:15), he appointed his sons over Israel. On what basis were his sons appointed? We aren't told. But it was the people, again, who confirmed to Samuel that his sons were wicked and did evil. The people wanted to bypass the structure of using judges and instead asked for a king to be appointed (1 Sam 8:2–6).

Chapter Summary

Leadership expectations are culturally shaped by the society. Jesus challenged the cultural assumptions of power in leadership by modeling and teaching the character of servanthood to his disciples. Paul taught Titus that leaders emerge from successful and loving leadership in their families. The unfaithful leadership of the sons of Eli and Samuel illustrate that leadership can be either affirmed or challenged by those who are to be led; it is not a right of succession.

Leadership also requires wisdom that can analyze, synthesize, and evaluate new information before offering a vision for the future and choosing the right paths to move the community forward in manners that harmonize with the communities expectations of pace and flexibility.

Preparing leaders is a task of God the Father, according to Jesus' explanation to the mother of James and John. It begins with providential experiences, such as the future King David fighting a lion and a bear as a shepherd boy. Leadership can be taught effectively using stories of both successful and unsuccessful examples from the Bible.

Part 3

Implementing Curriculum Design Remedies

Chapter 10

Design Elements that Counteract Negative Influences

As first presented in the Introduction, "curriculum" can be translated as "path" and communicates the choices an educator will make to cause another to learn. Education is not a "pure" discipline; it is derived and built from anthropological, psychological, and sociological foundations. Educators use observations from those sciences and study how man best learns and suggest educational activities that provide remedies to those different obstacles challenging learning. Part 2 identified many of those obstacles derived from questions and information from those academic disciplines. Academic disciplines are not powerful because of the mountains of data they provide, but because of the perspectives and questions those disciplines provide that produce the data. The different perspectives they use to observe man is then applied by an educator to create the best practices to cause learning.

This chapter suggests educational activities that counteract the seven potentially negative influences described in the previous chapters. The design decisions don't change the bible story/lesson *content*—that never changes—but address the *process* of how the content is presented to ever-enlarging networks of people. The design decisions appearing under each negative influence can also be used as helpful evaluation tools to help you evaluate your current learning approaches.

The Influence of Unmatched Teaching and Learning Preferences

1. Concepts should be taught adaptively in visual, dramatic, constructive, musical, or storytelling formats common to the learner's culture.

2. Stories should not be delivered in a style that restricts the ability of the new believer to repeat the same style to another.

The Influence of the Listener's Own Worldview

3. The lesson is based upon a story or illustrates a biblical principle.
4. The lesson relates to the listener's own worldview.
5. The lesson encourages the listeners to place themselves into the story to consider personal applications.
6. The lesson identifies ideas that can reflect a challenge to an existing worldview.
7. The lesson is not disrespectful of the culture's worldview, but provides an alternative (biblical) perspective.
8. The lesson presents a clear contrast between the existing worldview and the biblical kingdom worldview.
9. The lesson encourages the choice to resolve the problems presented by the existing worldview, leading to adopting the preferred worldview (applying conceptual change teaching strategy).
10. The lesson is sensitive to the issues of honor and shame, guilt and innocence, purity and pollution, or fear and power held by the listener.

The Influence of the Storyteller Assuming the Role of Teacher

11. The lesson is heavily reliant upon the use of questions to encourage dialogue.
12. The lesson encourages listener discovery rather than the teacher declaring the point of the lesson.
13. The lesson encourages immediate response and commitment to action or change.
14. The lesson begins with accountability for responses from the previous lesson.
15. The lesson is respectful of the listener and reduces the difference between the roles of teacher and student and encourages equality in the relationship.

The Influence of Addition Instead of Multiplication Processes

Design Elements that Counteract Negative Influences

16. A multiplication strategy depends upon lessons that enable new believers quickly re-tell biblical stories to personal friends, both new believers and unbelievers.
17. The lesson requires no additional resources, being dependent upon memory and oral telling.
18. The lesson is suitable for evangelism or discipleship of a new believer.
19. The lesson can be taught by new disciples within the community and not dependent upon teachers outside the community.
20. The lesson, being simple, short, memorable, and contextually independent, requires no prior Christian background.
21. The lesson is not different than the learning style within the community.

The Influence of Restricting Movement Growth

22. The lesson is simple, short, and memorable so it is easily transferable.
23. The lesson is written to reach "the others" (the fourth generation) and not just the "Paul's" (the first generation) in reference to 2 Timothy 2:2. (Our objective is a lesson that can be told simply by someone we haven't and probably won't ever meet. It must therefore be able to be easily and fully repeatable.)
24. The lesson has no more than three or four points. (Create another lesson if more points are needed.)
25. The lesson relies on few scriptures with no supporting cross-references.
26. The lesson is designed to encourage a group relationship through group discussion.
27. The lesson is non-confrontational or threatening so it can be used with close friends or family.

The Influence of Diverse Beliefs and Practices within the Culture

28. The lesson is consistent in the time required to conduct, prepare, study, complete, and apply the lesson objectives.
29. The lesson times meet consistently for the same length of time.
30. The lesson is preferably held at the same location and the same time.
31. The lesson is presented in a consistent format. Consistency in every area of the story lesson, including the scheduling pattern and the process of thought and creativity, is critical to reduce confusion and

PART 3 : IMPLEMENTING CURRICULUM DESIGN REMEDIES

reinforce the model. Lessons that are consistent in their schedule and process make it easier to develop a personal habit of study and models how to conduct a study for the others down the spiritual generational line. This helps the growing story communities to identify with each other by doing the same things the same way. Athletes refer to doing the same actions the same way as developing "muscle memory," which means the muscles respond the same way for every athletic action. To create a culture requires developing the same kind of mental memory that can reproduce and multiply itself so the consistency of the study patterns keeps the movement unified. Consistency also applies to the process of crafting the story. If you follow the same process, such as the seven components of each story as presented in the next section, you will find this will help maintain a consistent "sound and feel" to each story.

The Influence of Leadership Using Local but Unbiblical Criteria

32. The lesson's learning objective is realized when the listener can apply the information to change understanding or to respond appropriately to similar situations.
33. The lesson's learning objective is realized when responses enable leaders to analyze and apply lessons to illustrate and communicate vision, provide insight toward spiritual growth, or create solutions to community issues.

The Relationship of Curriculum Design and Story Lessons

Suggesting that thirty-two curriculum design elements must be applied to tell story lessons contradicts the importance of simplicity to support reproduction! But these elements only guide the story crafter in the initial design of the story. After that, the finished stories continue through generations of storytelling without intentionally being aware of each design decision. Consider the curriculum decisions made with crafting a sermon or writing a book or pamphlet. Those decisions are only made one time; they don't need to be repeated each time the sermon or book is reproduced. The model established the lesson and, similarly, the same story craftsmanship.

Moreover, the relationship of the curriculum design remedies to counteract the negative influences is simplified in the following summary:

Design Elements that Counteract Negative Influences

Education Strategies

1. Mismatched teaching and learning preferences.

   Description: Teachers often teach using a literate style with learners who prefer an oral learning style. A preferred learning style describes how we prefer to receive, process, remember, and repeat information. Literate cultures prefer printed text; oral cultures do not. As many as 80 percent of the world are oral-preference learners!

   Remedy: Teach in agreement with majority learning preference, which is often oral.

2. Persistence of the listeners' pre-existing unbiblical worldview.

   Description: All people construct their personal view of how the world works. Because new information is always linked and built upon previous information, new information is often interpreted according to the listener's existing beliefs.

   Remedy: Present new information using the four steps of the conceptual change teaching strategy. Because all worldviews are personally constructed, they cannot be changed by anyone else, therefore new material must engage the listener to question existing beliefs.

3. Storyteller assumes the role of authoritative teacher.

   Description: When a storyteller adds information outside the story itself or declares the meaning of the story, the teller becomes the authoritative source instead of the story itself. Additional material also confuses the ability to repeat the story to following generations.

   Remedy: The storyteller—no matter his experience or maturity—must remain a facilitator who uses questions and discussion to enable the listener to discover the meaning from the story.

Reproduction Strategies

4. Defaulting to addition ministry processes.

   Description: Depending on the evangelist or discipler to be the primary or only source for storytelling is using an addition process.

   Remedy: All evangelists or disciplers must replace themselves with new converts to multiply disciplers, requiring the curriculum to be simple, short, memorable, and easily repeatable.

Part 3 : Implementing Curriculum Design Remedies

5. Restricting movement growth.

   Description: Limiting new believers from evangelism and discipling ministries in favor of permitting discipleship only to mature believers.

   Remedy: Evangelism should spread rapidly through personal relational networks so new believers must continue to disciple other new believers, requiring discipleship to continue to emerge simply through biblical stories.

Community Strategies

6. Permitting a variety of different theological and practices to emerge within the community.

   Description: Permitting different Christian practices allows divisions within the community that should be establishing its culture and enabling mutual accountability to theology and behaviors criteria among its members.

   Remedy: Develop habits that support behaviors, including Bible storytelling, and beliefs that the movement wants to reinforce and maintain through mutual accountability.

7. Relying on unbiblical local leadership concepts when appointing leaders.

   Description: Every culture has leadership that has both functional and character requirements. The new Christian community cannot choose leaders based upon non-biblical requirements.

   Remedy: Identify the functional leadership requirements of the culture, but recognize the new leaders are called and appointed by God as they display commitment to biblical character requirements.

A careful reading of these proposed curriculum decisions will reveal they are quite common and unremarkable; not one suggestion is radical, distinctive, innovative, or complex. Their simple and ordinary character is what makes their implementation easy and painless to adopt. But what makes their implementation profound is understanding their purpose to affect negative influences and why they must be intentionally applied within the story's presentation. It should sensitize the storyteller to recognize the subtle and dramatic implications when such educational remedies are ignored or minimized.

For example, what implications must be solved when the listener's skills and learning preferences are oral but the teacher/mentor/discipler is

Design Elements that Counteract Negative Influences

reliant on a literate preference and teaches to that preference? An implication is that the process won't be natural for the listener to imitate and therefore won't be shared even though the listener may agree with everything heard. That inability to repeat what was modeled stops the generational reproduction.

What implications must be solved if the stories are lengthy, complex, or detailed? These story lessons will require extensive memorization, which often discourages new believers' confidence that they would be able to repeat and defend the stories and discussions.

What implications must be solved to prevent new listeners from interpreting everything that is being told as part of his or her existing worldview? Without solving that issue, the person will walk away with a new story that is added to their existing beliefs or, at best, simply moved beliefs into a new syncretism.

These and other implications must be considered and solved using educational approaches. Storytelling is so much more than merely repeating stories! But what is being argued here is *not* that oral storying is the best, or even the only way of teaching. Rather, the argument is that curriculum design decisions affect which learners are included or excluded and, depending on the context, will affect the effectiveness of the strategy and goals of your ministry.

Chapter Summary

The seven negative influences working against generational reproduction can be counteracted by making appropriate educational decisions. Though thirty-two curriculum design elements were suggested, there is still simplicity in the process because those elements don't need to be taught along with the story to listeners. Only the story and lesson crafters must understand and make these decisions. The implications of learning needs and preferences must influence the curriculum decisions made by the lesson crafter because there is always a relationship between the ministry strategy, the learning characteristics of the people being reached, and the implications of the outreach strategy. How the story lesson is educationally designed and crafted must always consider how the learning preference of the listener and the mission strategy relate to each other.

Chapter 11

Teaching This Approach to Others

TELLING A BIBLICAL STORY lesson to one listener at a time is not the primary objective. The primary objective is creating spiritual generations that multiply, leading to a self-sustaining movement that grows using biblical story lessons. Using biblical story lessons is a powerful strategy because they are a natural, effective way to encourage and enable believers to create their own spiritual generations among their friends and personal networks using whatever little they know ("whether He is a sinner, I do not know; one thing I do know, that, whereas I was blind, now I see," John 9:25). The stories totally rely on authoritative Scripture that can answer the questions of any culture. Scripture not only commands us repeatedly to tell God's stories, but also uses the prophets and disciples—and Jesus himself—to tell stories to teach. Therefore, we can be assured that telling biblical stories of God's activities and works will be blessed.

Stories are a *method*, not the *objective*, and the method is simple yet powerful. The biblical story curriculum is within reach of not only the youngest convert, but even among those who are not believers. Telling biblical stories does not require a certain theological knowledge threshold, but storytellers must be able to cause others to learn through facilitating reflection and discussions. And with each story lesson being told, the potential of a longer spiritual lineage being carried into next generations increases.

The Two Groups in Your Generational Lineage

The first group in your own spiritual lineage are new believers who responded to the biblical stories. These believers are your "Timothy generation," who,

Teaching This Approach to Others

hopefully, will find "faithful men" among their friends to whom they can tell their stories. They do not need to be taught about the potential seven negative influences or the curriculum design decisions. They only need to repeat the biblical stories and lessons as told to them. They can multiply your lineage because they can replace you as the first-generation storyteller.

Those first new believers are invaluable sources of information for you. Not only can they reach their friends to share stories, but they are the best resource to provide the cultural insights that reveal their misconceptions that should be prioritized according to their critical influence and therefore address your priority in telling new stories. These would be familiar of their local storytelling forms including the words, the pacing, and their story style. I once developed a list of stories to present a chronological understanding of the Bible as requested by a new believer. But he became so frustrated with his unbelieving anti-Christian wife that he wanted to divorce her. That redirected my priorities to develop stories about the biblical covenant of marriage which had been minimized by his own religious background.

New believers' responses also provide insight how others would interpret the stories from their own cultural worldview. They may be reluctant to share or are unable to communicate the differences between their cultural and biblical understandings so, more likely, you will gather more information from intentionally listening to off-hand comments.

But a second group of "Timothys" must also develop—those old and new believers who are able and motivated to craft stories to teach the storytellers. Unlike the storytellers, these crafters must thoroughly understand and apply these curriculum design principles. Gather small crafting teams of three to five members who hold the same vision and commitment to work with each other regularly to craft story lessons appropriate to their cultural needs and that challenge faulty worldviews. These people do not need to be from the fringes of the world, but could form within the local, established church. These teams should be closest to the needs and attitudes of the community; in fact, it would be preferable to select those from among the community itself. They will provide the critical words, phrases, and points of identification with the listeners that will make the stories relevant and soaring. This group, if possible, will produce story lessons that summarize all seven components of the lesson format on a single sheet of paper and categorized, or grouped, according to topics.

PART 3 : IMPLEMENTING CURRICULUM DESIGN REMEDIES

These new story crafters will bring their own misconceptions about biblical storying with them, and there will be those in the Christian community whose support may be questionable or lukewarm. The most common misconception you will face is that stories are childish and are inappropriate for "real" or "advanced" education. But you now recognize how powerful, sophisticated, and accessible storying can be. A second misconception is that storying is only for passing on information. But you now recognize that the story can influence people to change their way of looking at how the world works; it's beyond simply knowing information. A third misconception is that storying is only used as an evangelism tool for unbelievers, but true discipleship requires more training in doctrinal categories. But you now appreciate that biblical stories are a method of teaching spiritual behaviors and habits to be put into practice and that it is important for the listeners to have a part in constructing their doctrinal categories from the Scripture they hear. A fourth misconception is that telling the story is all that is required, but you now appreciate the value of preparing to facilitate discussions about the story as a means of gaining insight into your listeners' worldviews. You also will witness the impact of interaction that produces and unfolds the discovery of truth for the listener. A fifth common misconception is that the story can be told by simply memorizing the story, but you now recognize the necessity of working hard to craft the stories themselves to make them short, easily reproduced, and memorable so that others are able to retell the stories.

As you meet these common objections or misconceptions directly, you will also need to eliminate misconceptions about the vision of the team. Addressing these misconceptions is a constant process of listening carefully and providing clarification. For comparison, recall how long it took the disciples to understand Jesus' vision. Even he expressed amazement at how long it took them to understand!

Everyone on your crafting team likely partnered with you by agreeing with *some* aspect of your vision that agreed with their personal vision of ministry. It is probable that they didn't agree with *every* aspect of your vision because they interpreted what they heard from you according to their own vision. Therefore, describe your vision not only by what it is, but by what it is not—and what it is not will only become apparent through discussion and restatements. For example, there will likely be at least one member of your team who agreed to your vision without recognizing the critical differences between being a teacher and a storyteller. Most teachers have

Teaching This Approach to Others

years of experience using (and modeling) a style based upon delivering information to persuade a student to arrive at the "right" answer so they can also teach others to arrive at the same conclusion. Another team member might have enthusiastically agreed to join because of a shared commitment to see the gospel spread, but failed to recognize that the strategy used in this approach is built upon first- and second-generation believers sharing with their non-believing relational networks. The educational, reproduction, and community strategies associated with the vision must often be restated as each new misconception becomes apparent.

These new members may come from literate backgrounds—even this book is in a literate format! Therefore, the logical order of the book and the material was presented for literate information processing. You are at liberty and encouraged to change the book material to fit the needs and preferences of your teammates' learning preferences.

Expect to be challenged by those who bring their own style from literate experiences. Learning new information always goes through three stages in the same order: rejection, toleration, and adoption. Not everyone makes it through all the stages and certainly not in an immediate time frame. Some people might take mere seconds to tolerate the ideas while others may take years, if they ever do. Don't be surprised! To meet objections, return to the biblical stories that were used to identify each problem and discuss the principles of the story together.

If too much information is taught unnecessarily or too early, it will violate the principle of keeping it simple, short, memorable, and easily reproducible. To keep the movement continuing, this second group of story crafters are those who know how and why to craft stories, but the information you teach this team must also be presented to them when necessary and appropriate.

If possible, safe, and appropriate, each story lesson outline—covering all seven sections of the story format (misconception, main points, biblical passage, story, questions, Scripture memory, and hook question)—should be summarized on a single sheet of paper. However, be very cautious that these written stories are not passed on to the storytellers so they aren't influenced in their telling by the literate mindset and emphasis of the written words. If they are shared with other storytellers beyond your immediate culture, also be extremely cautious so the error of creating stories for one culture are wholly imported into another culture that has a different set of values, learning preferences, attitudes, or issues.

PART 3 : IMPLEMENTING CURRICULUM DESIGN REMEDIES

Identifying Your Listener Target Groups

Good curriculum is learner centered rather than teacher centered. This book has emphasized changes in teaching strategies because many teachers or disciplers naturally model their styles and teaching techniques from literate-reliant teachers and have not experienced or seen a non-literate approach according to the learner's and not teacher's preference. Not all people who prefer oral storying are from unreached, foreign oral-preference cultures; they are all around us.

We all have learned how to adapt to different styles of teaching that don't always align with our learning preference. But our goal is for new listeners to retell story lessons in their relationships and the likelihood of that happening will increase if we model a teaching strategy that most closely fits their personal learning preference. Oral stories should fit the character and goals for the ministry group you are trying to penetrate with God's stories to create spiritual generations within each group.

Evaluate your ministry opportunities to apply storying strategy and curriculum design that could benefit those ministries in which you're already engaged or to reach new people. Consider how your evangelism or discipleship practices might change using the educational design principles presented in this book. How could they help, in particular, oral learners or those who will be ministering to oral-preference learners? How could they be applied to children, youth, international students, refugees and immigrants, prisoners, and unreached people groups? How could you apply some, if not all, of these design principles to initiate outreach movements among your ministry targets? What would you do differently?

Obviously, you would craft stories differently for children to learn and share with their friends than you would for adults. Children learn through play and listening to stories and begin to form their worldviews from what works for them or gives them pleasure. They love to assume character roles of any story, whether the hero, the villain, or someone with whom they can identify. The objective for Bible storytellers is to have children build their worldviews biblically and tell stories to their childhood friends. Children are concrete thinkers; when younger, they do not have the capability of thinking through abstract thoughts such as principles. There is no expectation that they understand misconceptions, but they are used to hearing stories and then retelling them. Therefore, the objective is that they learn stories that are simple and straightforward and can relate to their world.

Teaching This Approach to Others

Children enjoy making close friends, so forming "story clubs" or even "story minutes" within an existing childhood program would be fruitful for learning and practicing with each other. Practicing to tell stories in a presentation before parents or a Christian fellowship would be an encouragement to them and to the listeners. If oral storytelling is a valued skill for a missionary, there is certainly foundational value to becoming familiar with the traditions and rituals of the stories that shape their culture beginning in childhood.

Youth become exposed to new and competing philosophies and religions or worldviews, therefore it is a time to return to the foundational stories of their childhood though now asking questions of those stories that enable recognition between the worldviews exposed to them and a biblical worldview. This is not the time to rely on sermons and lectures, but rather on biblical stories that remain simple, short, memorable, and relevant for them to share with their friends. Now is the time to recognize that the stories learned were not simply part of children's stories that don't have relevance to their maturing adult lives. Rather than becoming irrelevant, the stories show their value as they speak to the principles and values needed in discerning truth and growing into a new, adult world.

International students are the best and brightest students of their nations. Therefore, during their short exposure to Christian understanding in a culture perhaps permitting greater religious freedom, the approach of evangelicals often matches their intellectual giftedness with offers of Christian books and philosophical discussions and debate with love and respect. This is the model of evangelism that, if they come to faith, they will take back to their country.

But what if their home countries are inhospitable to Christians? Will international students be permitted to return with Bibles and Christian literature to non-Christian countries hostile to Christian faith? Will they have access to Christian literature? Will they be able to model a safe and effective approach for evangelism and discipleship that they can use with oral-preference countrymen? Will they be able to reproduce spiritual generations in their homeland through literate-based methods? Will they have experience in leading discussions based upon biblical stories?

From discussions with others invested in international student ministry, a great challenge in the ministry is following up and encouraging these new believing students back in their homeland. Perhaps this is because oral learning and teaching wasn't modeled, giving deference to their literate

Part 3 : Implementing Curriculum Design Remedies

preference in learning. Modeling how to tell stories outside their countries may remove dependency on literate materials and provide confidence to the new believer who returns home without dangerous inventory to be confiscated at customs or remaining in their home for later distribution. Oral storytelling is a transferable method that can multiply in the home culture.

Current estimates report at least 250 million people are no longer living in their homeland. Therefore, the potential for providing for these refugees and immigrants living in local neighborhoods in host countries is growing more likely. For local churches to minister to these new strangers and aliens in their neighborhoods can be intimidating to believers who believe they must first be able to know different cultures, world religions, and how to defend their Christian faith and doctrine—and to do all of that with confidence, grace, and hospitality.

Storytellers should shed the pressure of those expectations; they are not expected to assume the role of a theologian able to discuss world religions. Of course the more that is known, the better the story may relate to the listener in order to raise probable misconceptions. But such knowledge is not *essential* to building relationships and sharing biblical stories with foreigners. The foreign listener already knows about his or her culture and religion—and knows more about it then the storyteller ever could. For the storyteller to presume to tell the foreigners about their own beliefs is insulting and may generate resentment. The storyteller is only responsible to tell the story he or she knows and encourage discussion about it with the listener. That's the extent of the expectation; tell a Bible story.

Some refugees and immigrants may be members of unreached people groups who are defined as lacking a self-sustaining church for the people of the group. God has strategically brought many of these people from hostile areas to be in a foreign situation where they expect to meet new and different cultures and where Christianity can be openly discussed, unlike their homeland. The value of storying is that it is not a hostile approach that creates suspicion of a desire to force conversion in a new and frightening land. Rather, it can be used to help introduce others to help them understand the religion of their new country.

Prison and jail ministries, or "the church inside," would benefit from using oral-preference biblical stories. Their population holds to a very different culture than those serving from the outside. The practice of discussions using questions rather than providing a sermon will communicate dignity to those who have lost respect. The Scriptures have much to say about prisoners that would resonate well and their situation and listeners would have opportunity to share stories with others.

Everything a believer shares with a listener becomes the model of how the listener approaches their own network of friends. Therefore, the kindness shown in simply presenting a Bible story is how each listener can model storytelling to another. Challenging misconceptions happens individually because our worldview is built and owned by each of us. Arguing or defending a position is not an attractive model for a person of peace within that community to share with others. Keep the biblical story the focal point of all discussions.

Final Words

So how was your curriculum path? Was the passing scenery sufficient with encouragements and warnings? As was challenged earlier, you make the choices because your community is different than mine. Those differences will lead to different discoveries and my prayer is that your resulting generations will bring joy to you and glory to our Savior.

Identify your ministry opportunities and gather a small group of friends within your church or missions agency and—together—begin to craft stories relevant to your context. Such storytelling communities could use encouragement, guidance, or on-site training and could share stories useful to other similar cultural outreaches. Therefore, I've created a new Web address for an online community of those who want to begin or improve their storytelling outreach. Visit anytime at www.StoriesThatMultiply.com and see what is available and, perhaps, useful to you.

Bibliography

Addison, Steve. *Movements that Change the World: Five Keys to Spreading the Gospel.* Downers Grove, IL: InterVarsity, 2011.

Allen, Roland. *The Spontaneous Expansion of the Church: And the Causes Which Hinder It.* Jawbone Digital, 2012.

Bains, Gurnek. *Cultural DNA: The Psychology of Globalization.* Hoboken, NJ: Wiley, 2015.

Biddell, T. R., et al. *Model Building: Toward a Constructivist Theory of Learning.* Paper presented at American Education Research Association, Chicago, April 1985. ERIC ED 271 203.

Bowman, K. Carla, with James Bowman. *Building Bridges to Oral Cultures: Journeys among the Least-Reached.* Pasadena, CA: William Carey Library, 2017.

Chiang, Samuel E., and Grant Lovejoy, eds. *Beyond Literate Western Models: Contextualizing Theological Education in Oral Contexts.* Hong Kong: International Orality Network, 2013.

Cron, Lisa. *Wired for Story: The Writer's Guide to Using Brain Science to Hook Readers from the Very First Sentence.* New York: Ten Speed, 2012.

Dear, John. *The Questions of Jesus: Challenging Ourselves to Discover Life's Great Answers.* New York: Doubleday, 2004.

DeSilva, David. *Honor, Patronage, Kinship and Purity: Unlocking New Testament Culture.* Downers Grove, IL: InterVarsity, 2000.

Duarte, Nancy. *Resonate: Present Visual Stories that Transform Audiences.* Hoboken, NJ: Wiley, 2010.

Duhigg, Charles. *The Power of Habit: Why We Do What We Do in Life and Business.* New York: Random House, 2012.

Foehr, Ulla. *Media Multitasking among American Youth: Prevalence, Predictors and Pairings.* National Education Association, 2006. https://www.kff.org/wp-content/uploads/2013/01/7592.pdf.

Koukl, Gregory. *Tactics: A Game Plan for Discussing Your Christian Convictions.* Grand Rapids: Zondervan. 2009.

Kutner, M., E. Greenberg, Y. Jin, B. Boyle, Y. Hsu, and E. Dunleavy. *Literacy in Everyday Life: Results from the 2003 National Assessment of Adult Literacy.* NCES 2007-480. U.S. Department of Education. Washington, DC: National Center for Education Statistics, 2007.

Lovejoy, Grant. "The Extent of Orality: 2012 Update." *Orality Journal* 1/1 (2012) 17.

Madinger, Charles. "A Literate's Guide to the Oral Galaxy." *Orality Journal* 2/2 (2013) 15.

Bibliography

Maloney, Jennifer. "The Fastest-Growing Format in Publishing: Audiobooks." *Wall Street Journal*, July 21, 2016.

Marshall, I Howard. *The Gospel of Luke: A Commentary on the Greek Text*. Grand Rapids: Eerdmans, 1978.

Mischke, Werner. *The Global Gospel: Achieving Missional Impact in Our Multicultural World*. Scottsdale, AZ: Mission ONE, 2015.

Muller, Roland. *Honor & Shame: Unlocking the Door*. Exlibris, 2000.

National Center for Education Statistics. *Fast Facts: Adult Literacy*. Organization for Economic Cooperation and Development, 2012. https://nces.ed.gov/fastfacts/display.asp?id=69.

National Endowment of the Arts. *To Read or Not to Read: A Question of National Consequence*. Research Report 47. 2007. https://www.arts.gov/sites/default/files/ToRead.pdf.

Richards, E. Randolph, and Brandon J. O'Brien. *Misreading Scripture with Western Eyes*. Downers Grove, IL: InterVarsity, 2012.

Ripken, Nik, and Gregg Lewis. *The Insanity of God: A True Story of Faith Resurrected*. Nashville: B&H, 2013.

Roché, James A., Jr. *Conceptual Change Problems in Theological Learning*. EdD diss., Trinity Evangelical Divinity School, 1991.

Schattner, Frank Walter. *Sustainability within Church Planting Movements in East Asia*. PhD diss., Cook School of Intercultural Studies, Biola University, 2013.

Smith, Steve, and Ying Kai. *T4T: A Discipleship Re-Revolution*. Monument, CO: WIGTake Resources, 2011.

Steffen, Tom. *Worldview-Based Storying: The Integration of Symbol, Story, and Ritual in the Orality Movement*. Richmond, VA: Orality Resources International, Center for Oral Scriptures, 2018.

Tennent, Timothy. *Theology in the Context of World Christianity*. Grand Rapids: Zondervan, 2007.

Terry, J. O. *Basic Bible Storying: Preparing and Presenting Bible Stories for Evangelism, Discipleship, Training and Ministry*. Fort Worth, TX: Church Starting Network, 2008.

Vella, Jane. *Learning to Listen, Learning to Teach: The Power of Dialogue in Educating Adults*. San Francisco: Jossey-Bass, 1994.

Walsh, John D. *The Art of Storytelling: Easy Steps to Presenting an Unforgettable Story*. Chicago: Moody, 2014.

Ward, Ted, Lois Mikinney-Douglas, and John Detoni. "Effective Learning in Nonformal Modes." *Common Ground Journal* 11/1 (Fall 2013) 32.

Wu, Jackson. *One Gospel for All Nations: A Practical Approach to Biblical Contextualization*. Pasadena, CA: William Carey Library, 2015.

———. *Saving God's Face: A Chinese Contextualization of Salvation through Honor and Shame*. Pasadena, CA: William Carey International University Press, 2012.

Zull, James E. *The Art of Changing the Brain: Enriching Teaching by Exploring the Biology of Learning*. Sterling, VA: Stylus, 2002.

Scripture Index

(All references are from the NASB version)

Genesis 3:7,8	56	John 9:17–25	96, 126
Exodus 12:14–28	39	John 14:11	41
Leviticus 19:13–18	65	John 15:18–21	108
Deuteronomy 6:4,5	65	John 16:7	82
Deuteronomy 31:9–11	37, 38	John 17:4	83
Joshua 2:9–13	40–41	John 17:18	83
1 Samuel 2:12,34	114	Acts 2:41	78
1 Samuel 3:20	114	Acts 2:47	78
1 Samuel 7:15	114	Acts 4:4	78
1 Samuel 8:2–6	115	Acts 5:14	78
1 Samuel 17:34–37	114	Acts 5:41	108
2 Kings 22:3–23:3	38	Acts 12:11–17	79
Psalms 71:17–18	39	Acts 15:23	79
Psalms 78:1–7, 9–10	39, 40	Romans 15:4	11, 39
Psalms 118:22	106	Romans 12:2	68
Psalms 145:4–7, 11–12	xvii, 40	1 Corinthians 1:13–2:5	101
Ecclesiastes 4:9–10	105	1 Corinthians 2:1, 4–5	43
Matthew 5:21–32	55	Ephesians 4:17–19	107
Matthew 13:1–13	48, 49, 52, 79		
Matthew 20:25–28	110	2 Timothy 2:2	xiv, 14, 37, 121
Matthew 23:8, 11–12	53, 73	2 Timothy 3:16–17	xv, 7, 11, 13, 20
Matthew 24:9	108	Titus 1:5	113
Mark 2:14–16	87	Hebrews 1:1	39

Scripture Index

Mark 5:1–20	*88*	Hebrews 4:12	*19*
Mark 10:17–23	*64*	Hebrews 10:24–25	*105*
Mark 10:45	*107*	Hebrews 12:2	*106*
Luke 5:27–30	*87*	1 Peter 2:7	*106*
Luke 10:5–7	*87*	1 Peter 4:3–4,14–15	*63–64,78*
Luke 10:25–37	*64, 66, 67*	1 Peter 4:12	*108*
John 4:5–30,39,41–42	*90*	3 John 4	*83*

www.ingramcontent.com/pod-product-compliance
Lightning Source LLC
Chambersburg PA
CBHW070907160426
43193CB00011B/1399